SERIES A

Charles W. F. Smith
and
Helmut Koester

FORTRESS PRESS Philadelphia, Pennsylvania

Table of Contents

Library of Congress Catalog Card Number 74-76925

ISBN 0-8006-4063-2

Second Printing 1975

5365H75 Printed in U.S.A. 1-4063

General Preface

Proclamation: Aids for Interpreting the Lessons of the Church Year is a series of twenty-six books designed to help clergymen carry out their preaching ministry. It offers exegetical interpretations of the lessons for each Sunday and many of the festivals of the church year, plus homiletical ideas and insights.

The basic thrust of the series is ecumenical. In recent years the Episcopal church, the Roman Catholic church, the United Church of Christ, the Christian Church (Disciples of Christ), the United Methodist Church, the Lutheran and Presbyterian churches, and also the Consultation on Church Union have adopted lectionaries that are based on a common three-year system of lessons for the Sundays and festivals of the church year. *Proclamation* grows out of this development, and authors have been chosen from all of these traditions. Some of the contributors are parish pastors; others are teachers, both of biblical interpretation and of homiletics. Ecumenical interchange has been encouraged by putting two persons from different traditions to work on a single volume, one with the primary responsibility for exegesis and the other for homiletical interpretation.

Despite the high percentage of agreement between the traditions, both in the festivals that are celebrated and the lessons that are appointed to be read on a given day, there are still areas of divergence. Frequently the authors of individual volumes have tried to take into account the various textual traditions, but in some cases this has proved to be impossible; in such cases we have felt constrained to limit the material to the Lutheran readings.

The preacher who is looking for "canned sermons" in these books will be disappointed. These books are one step removed from the pulpit: they explain what the lessons are saying and suggest ways of relating this biblical message to the contemporary situation. As such they are springboards for creative thought as well as for faithful proclamation of the word.

The editor-homiletician of this volume of *Proclamation* is Charles W. F. Smith, Professor Emeritus, Episcopal Theological School, Cambridge, Mass., and the exegete is Helmut Koester, John H. Morrison Professor of New Testament Studies and Winn Professor of Ecclesiastical History,

Harvard Divinity School, Cambridge, Mass. Dr. Smith was born in England and received his basic education in that country before coming to the United States where he attended university and seminary. After graduating from the Episcopal Theological Seminary in Alexandria, Va., he served Christ Church, Exeter, N.H., for six years before returning to the Washington area where he was canon chancellor of Washington Cathedral and also instructor in homiletics at the Episcopal Theological Seminary, Alexandria, Va. In 1945 he became rector of St. Andrew's Episcopal Church in Wellesley, Mass., and shortly thereafter also lecturer in homiletics at Episcopal Theological Seminary, Cambridge, Mass. From 1951-1973 he was professor of New Testament at this same school. Dr. Smith has published books both in the area of preaching and New Testament studies. His most recent book is *The Paradox of Jesus in the Gospels.* Dr. Koester, the exegete, is a native of Germany and a graduate of the University of Marburg. Following his ordination he obtained an assistantship and later on an assistant professorship in the field of New Testament studies at the University of Heidelberg. In 1958 he came to Harvard Divinity School as a visiting professor; he stayed on and now holds chairs in both New Testament studies and church history. He has published numerous articles on these subjects in learned journals and encyclopedias in the United States and Europe. In 1971 he published a series of essays with James Robinson entitled *Trajectories through Early Christianity.* He is the chairman of the New Testament Editorial Committee of *Hermeneia—A Critical and Historical Commentary on the Bible* and in this series he has edited Eduard Lohse, *Colossians and Philemon* (1971) and Martin Dibelius and Hans Conzelmann, *The Pastoral Epistles* (1972).

Ash Wednesday

Lutheran	Roman Catholic	Episcopal	Pres./UCC/Chr.	Methodist/COCU
Joel 2:12-19	Joel 2:12-18	Joel 2:12-19	Joel 2:12-18	Joel 2:12-19
2 Cor. 5:20-6:2	2 Cor. 5:20-6:2	2 Cor. 5:20b-6:10	2 Cor. 5:20-6:2	2 Cor. 5:20b-6:10
Matt. 6:1-6, 16-18 (19-21)	Matt. 6:1-6, 16-18	Matt. 6:1-6, 16-21	Matt. 6:1-6, 16-18	Matt. 6:1-6, 16-21

EXEGESIS

First Lesson: Joel 2:12–19. The Book of Joel was written in the late Persian period (4th century B.C.). The first chapter speaks of an actual devastation by an invasion of locusts and cries to the Lord for help in this disaster. Joel 2:1–11 announces the coming of the day of the Lord. An invincible apocalyptic army led by God himself approaches. Its arrival is seen as a terrible theophany in which even the cosmic order is reversed (2:10). Thus the hopeless question, "who [among the holy people of God] can endure it?"

Joel 2:12–19 is composed of two pieces in traditional liturgical style: (1) a call for public repentance (2:12–14), (2) instructions for the enactment of this call (2:15–17). The remaining verses (2:18–19) are the opening sentences of a new section that includes the famous verses about the pouring out of the Holy Spirit in the last days quoted in Acts 2:17 ff. (= Joel 2:28–32).

The call for public repentance opens with an explicit contrast to 2:1–11 ("Yet even now") and reflects the Deuteronomistic message of "turn back to the Lord." Fasting, weeping, and mourning are the rituals of repentance. Joel 2:13 criticizes the rending of garments; it is useless, if there is no renewal of thought and will ("heart"). Joel 2:13b cites a frequently quoted formula of confession (cf. Exod. 34:6; Ps. 86:15; especially Jonah 3:9) in order to give the motivation for the call to repentance; not the existing crisis but God's nature and will are the ultimate motivation for the conduct of the people (priestly torah) and for God's plans (prophetic torah). The freedom of God is preserved (2:14a). God's repentance would re-establish the fruitfulness of the land; cereal and drink offerings would be possible again (2:14b). This text is not anti-ritualistic at all, in spite of the "rend your hearts and not your garments." The right offering of the gifts would document the fact that peace and welfare have returned to the people through God's graciousness.

The instructions for the enactment (2:15–17) begin with a comprehensive listing of all the people—even women and children—for all are threatened by the destruction of the day of the Lord; cf. Joel 2:28 f. where the young and the old are also listed as recipients of the divine spirit. Bride and bridegroom are listed separately, since they are otherwise exempted from certain rituals. In 2:17 the cultic setting is again emphasized. In the prayer of repentance in this verse, instead of the RSV translation, read "possession" (instead of "heritage") and "ruled by the nations" (instead of "mocked among the nations"). The people's independent existence as such is threatened. But from the threat which is coming *from* the Lord, the people can only flee *to* the Lord. No particular "sin" or "immorality" is quoted. The motivation is rather the destruction that is always imminent if the people do not base their existence on an attitude that is constantly waiting for God's mercy.

It is questionable whether one should include 2:18–19, since it raises an entirely different perspective. Joel now speaks of the future and its bliss. The "jealousy" of God is no longer seen as a destructive power, but as a motivation for God to act and to re-establish the fruitfulness and security of the land. The promise of grain, wine, and oil looks back to Joel 1, the last phrase of 2:19 looks back to 2:1–11 and finds a further elaboration in 2:20.

Second Lesson: 2 Cor. 5:20–6:2. These verses belong to the first of the several letters which are now combined in our Second Letter to the Corinthians. In this letter (2 Cor. 2:14–6:13) Paul launches his first attack against the foreign super-apostles and miracle workers who had questioned his legitimacy as an apostle of Christ. Paul's defense is that he cannot and will not recommend himself through his great actions (cf. 2 Cor. 5:12), but that it is his message from which the Corinthians must derive the evidence of his legitimacy.

The lesson is the second half of a section that begins with 5:16. Its theme is: Christ is present only in the message of reconciliation, but not in any other thing that an apostle might do. "To know Christ according to the flesh" (5:16) apparently means a recognition of Christ's presence through a visible and tangible performance such as a miracle that an apostle might perform. This is excluded, because "in Christ" signifies a new creation (5:17a). The old things have passed away (5:17b); this is a radical judgment about everything that belongs to this age, including its religious values. This is more elaborately stated in the words of apocalyptic mythology in Rev. 21:1–7—an important illustration of the radical eschatological dimension of this verse.

In 5:18 Paul turns this eschatological statement into a functional anthropological sentence. The basis of this sentence is a traditional credal formula which Paul quotes in 5:19. The usual translation, "God was in Christ reconciling . . . ," is wrong; 5:19 must be translated in analogy to 5:18: "It was God who through Christ reconciled the world to himself." The point of this quotation is that the office of reconciliation, i.e., the apostle and his message, is part of the event of a cosmic act of reconciliation which changes the time from the old age to the new. "Reconciliation" is, of course, not understood as something that people could do in order to reconcile God. On the contrary, it is solely God's act of making peace, sacrificing his own rights and claims, and ending the enmity.

On behalf of God, as the messenger of the other party in this peacemaking activity, Paul requests that the people accept God's terms which are identical with the sacrifice of God's rights. The super-apostles in Corinth represent Christ's religious greatness and power, but Paul represents Christ's dying (cf. 2 Cor. 4:10 ff) through which the believers become "righteousness of God" (5:20–21). Since God himself reversed his role, gave up his rights, made Christ into sin, even though he knew of no sin, the apostle cannot do anything in his ministry that is great and glorious. But he is indeed a co-worker of God and he is legitimized, if that "grace" (that act of God's sacrifice on behalf of reconciliation) has not proven to be in vain, i.e., if the people have indeed now become reconciled to God (6:1). 6:2 introduces the quote of Isa. 49:8 which speaks of the eschatological salvation "now."

The opponents had challenged Paul's legitimacy in their attempt to test the truth of the Christian religion by the demonstration of personal greatness and power. In their opinion the church leader owed such a test to the people in order to verify the truth of his message. Paul states that such verification—because of the nature of the message—can only be given by those whom God wants to reconcile, by the people. The apostle as a person is nothing. Paul had expressed this most forcefully in his reference to Joel 2:11 in 2 Cor. 2:16: "Who can endure it?" (RSV translates "who is sufficient?"). Thus, this Second Lesson is closely related to the First Lesson from Joel 2. All that matters is that the people return to God and to his grace.

Gospel: Matt. 6:1–6, 16–18 (19–21). Matt. 6:1–18 is a part of the "sermon on the mount." This whole section treats critically the three main observances of the Jewish religion: almsgiving, praying, and fasting. These three themes occur in succession in 6:1–4, 5–15, and 16–18. The part on praying is almost completely left out here (except for 6:5–6), since it contains the Lord's prayer which presents special problems of interpretation. Matt. 6:19–21 relates to a different subject matter and will not be included here.

The composition of the section is the work of Matthew (Luke has no analogous passage). Matthew, however, has used older models: the Gospel of Thomas (Saying 62) and the Teaching of the Twelve Apostles contain parallel treatments of these three observances. The introduction in 6:1 is entirely from the hand of the Gospel writer (also 6:7). The rest is a loose composition of rules and maxims for religious observance which are completely within the horizon of enlightened Judaism of that time: not external observations are decisive, but the inner orientation of the heart, mind, and spirit. The prophetical tradition of the OT had emphasized this in many instances, and there are several examples from the Jewish tradition which make the same point. What goes somewhat beyond such Jewish observation is Matthew's repeated use of hyperbolic formulations, as in 6:3 and 17 (perhaps these are original words of Jesus). Their advice to create the opposite impression to those outside radicalizes religious observation to the point of absurdity.

"Righteousness" in 6:1 means specifically "almsgiving," but also recalls the word about the "better righteousness" (5:20). It contrasts with a behavior which wants to make its religious significance demonstrable. All that falls under the verdict "hypocrisy" (6:2; cf. 6:16). Everything must be done in secret, with no reward and no visible success, either personal or otherwise (6:4). This complete denial of the propaganda value of religious observances becomes even more obvious with respect to prayer. The quotation from Isa. 26:20 (Matt. 6:6) underlines this: prayer is an exercise of people in hiding while eschatological troubles overwhelm the world. With respect to fasting, there is no difference. "Dismal" looking people who fast want nothing more than to exhibit their religious seriousness (the word "dismal" is often used otherwise for the face that one presents to all sorts of serious and disastrous events). Christians have no business to share in the sorrows of the world by the exercise of "dismal" religious rites.

As a whole, this section of the sermon on the mount is not only an attack on religious customs and observances, whether or not they reflect an enlightened understanding of rituals and public religious actions.

What is said here amounts to a radical refusal to exhibit the validity of the Christian religion in a public demonstration. The "better righteousness" of the disciples of Jesus turns out to be the freedom of the fools of God—they are requested to fool everybody else when they give alms and pray and fast.

HOMILETICAL INTERPRETATION

Introduction. Ash Wednesday nowadays can seem an arbitrary appointment, and Lent an artificial arrangement. Fasting and penitence, if we are to understand Jesus, are not determined by dates on a calendar but by events or conditions (Mark 2:19a, and Joel). So Ash Wednesday can be the solemn (as distinct from dismal) entry into the recognition of the death and resurrection of Christ, providing a period of reflection on it and what led to it. The traditionally biblical "forty days" provide Sundays on which the preacher will try to give his people something to keep alive their special interest during the week.

First Lesson. The OT lessons do not always stress the element of judgment, so it is necessary (as the exegesis has done) to read them in book-context. Judgment is not an arbitrary act but is built-in in the process of history. "Even now"—the watchman-preacher tries to speak of the upcoming crises as well as of those we are presently involved in, anticipating (with the Spirit's help) the problems that will arise from the way we work through the present ones, the problems of the peace that will follow even the victory, the new crisis that will arise from the immediate adjustments made (the so-called solution), as the prophets did.

The judgment, each new "day of the Lord," is not heralded by the roar of planes, the rumble of tanks, the hiss of rockets, any more than it was by armies of locusts. These human upheavals may be signs but the basic issue is not settled when they are quieted. The most widely oppressive forms of violence are silent, socially approved, institutional. But God's footsteps are there and his judgments are the prelude to good news, retribution the preparation for redemption—*if the turn is made.*

The call to respond by turning is to the whole community of faith. In a pluralistic society the churches can be only minority witnesses and we must realize that. But a minority which points in a radically other direction can be a potent source of change. The call is for the relaxing of other claims so that this one may at once have priority. It can be symbolized by the relaxing of the claims of family, the fellowship of "bed and board." Not that the intimate associations of the home are wrong.

But, as with all our other institutions, they need the reinforcement of Christian fellowship, the scrutiny and grace which the broader "penumbra" of God's glory can provide.

The priests too are called to turn. The ministry must be the example. It is not "the world" that is called to "turn," but the church itself. Repentance is re-orientation, checking or entering upon a new direction, the taking of which requires a pause for locating oneself. For being "lost" is not inability to see where we are. Even in a fog we can see on what our feet stand. The need is to relate that spot to some more distant feature if we are to know "where we are at" in the sense, the all-important sense, of "where do we go from here?"

Ash Wednesday, Lent, can be such a pause, a means of checking the normally more distant landmarks of faith by which each single step is directed. So much of modern life is a mere stumbling from spot to spot, a lurching from side to side, a nose-to-the-ground nibbling from enticing tuft to tuft until, like sheep, we look up and find we are lost for lack of an eye to the flock, an open ear to the shepherd.

The important sense is, as Joel saw, that God is on the move already. The future event, the impending crisis, can be handled if we know God well enough now to be assured that he will be there before us, anticipating us. Lent is, then, a time to nurture this expectancy—and that expectancy should be one of the differences that marks us as Christians.

The orientation point is the cross, thrown into relief by the glory of the resurrection experience. We choose its shadow in full knowledge that this dark, certainly, is produced by the presence of that light. To bear the cross along our way is to reveal something of the compassion of God, known to us in the Christ who suffered by identification with those who were thrust aside by religious contemporaries. Lent is the turn into that way. "Even now."

Second Lesson. Joel's "even now" becomes Paul's quotation of Isaiah's "Now." This is the day. The immediacy of the gospel is to be stressed. It is not a device aimed at an eventual release into heaven. The future is now. Already it is a new age and new things are possible. A word heard, a page of history turned, a community crisis, an illness, a vow taken, can be the suddenly wide swinging door through which enters—God! The door then stays open on a new vista, into a new orientation, a new life for individual and congregation or community. For this the preacher must pray constantly and preach earnestly. There is no apostolic sign, only the new order at work, testified to in practice.

The immediate distance covered is from sin to righteousness, made possible by a journey "as far as the east is from the west." The instantaneous journey across the insurmountable was accomplished when (note the direction) the Holy became sin in Christ, so that we might know the reverse experience. It can begin in one of those experiences which happens in an instant but the implications of which cannot be grasped at once. The preacher will have homely instances, but the best are case-histories of Christians (St. Paul's is classic). The transforming power of such an experience can be worked out only across the years, during which we may come to doubt it ever took place. Yet it happened, and we must hold on to that fact, believe its reality, while we explore and rejoice in and realize in changed ways the outcome intended from the start. For the grace of God is not accepted for emptiness—just a note in an echo chamber, just a diploma to hang on a wall, just a hobby for the spare hour.

In what does the sudden opening-up, the new turn consist? "Reconciliation." But that is impossible without meeting, without a turning-towards. States which will not give recognition to each other's existence cannot achieve a peaceful *modus vivendi.* The alternative could be war which, by its nature, denies the worth of the enemy, their very existence as real people of like passions with ourselves. Enemies cannot enter into the joys, the expansion of personality to be found in fellowship. They cannot see each other, cannot speak, cannot touch. "The peace of the Lord be always with you" is not a liturgical change in the air-waves but the conviction of equal reality before God, by touch, by look, by words spoken and listened to, truly given, truly received. "Conciliation," like "toleration," can be demeaning. Reconciliation means willingness to *receive* understanding (how we shun it!), forgiveness if need be (how we dread it!), as well as to *give* it. To give it only is to be betrayed into Adam's mistake (see next Sunday) of wanting to play God, the pernicious idolatry of the self, our own identity preserved at all costs. Reconciliation, as Paul well knew, begins with being known. So God has taken the first step, making all other moves possible. He is the unknown Knower before he is the known. When we are known (loved) we can begin to know (to love). Reconciliation is to accept the knowing at the same time as we give it and to love can mean only the accepting of love.

There is an incapacitating "future shock" when God's end is not in view, no impact of the end-age experienced. But reconciliation is a condition experienced now, still "today." In winter, when the leaves are gone, the boundaries retire, the perspective lengthens and what is near-by seems more intimate, more immediate, somehow more urgent. This is the Christian realization that "now is the day." We, who we are, where we are, as we now are, who have now received the grace of God, cannot "let it go for nothing" (NEB). Being human is an entirely different matter for those who have the end in Christ in view. We are the reconciled: reconciled to time, to the present situation, to our condition as men and women, not by a shrugging of the shoulders acceptance, but by a dynamic new valuation of the whole situation. Redemption becomes the day of creation anew.

Gospel. The priority of turning toward God may be stressed at all levels, even in religious duties or disciplines. Otherwise the religious face we present to people is our own, for our instant gain, not theirs, not God's. To turn to God is also, in a sense, to turn away from religion, when religion is conceived as a pattern of formal exercises, noted and noticeable. Otherwise we have turned back to the world, inviting its recognition, general commendation, popular applause.

Strictly private! How astonishing (even if, as is said in the exegesis, there is a touch of hyperbole here)! The only private thing in gospel religion is religious practices. They are not matters for publicity. But what business would succeed without publicity? Christianity is not a business; we are not selling a product. Even the community's worship is not a public spectacle to be gaped at, applauded, staged as a wonder. It is to be participated in, individually and corporately at the same time, as a turning towards God, an orientation reaffirmed. What flows from it—works of charity, intercession, freedom to act by laying aside encumbrances—comes across without a name-tag, certainly without a price-tag, without a fanfared *leitmotif*, no photograph, no uniform. Religious exercises, personal, communal, are private in order that they may benefit all, not just us (1 Cor. 12:7, RSV). It is in the widening of results that our own spiritual health is established. To misuse religious exercises is to deprive ourselves of the real benefits they can and do bring to our spiritual life, to our growth in grace. The danger, otherwise, is the premature exhaustion of benefits: "They [already] have their reward." A sort of spiritual "built-in obsolescence." Dr. Oman, speaking to ministers, once said in effect, "A man cannot at the same time glorify himself and glorify his Lord."

But this does not make religious duties optional, even if they cannot be checked-up on. The manner in which we perform them may be (ought to be?) far from traditional and nearer to what we can interpret Jesus' way to be, presented as it is precisely to explain the ways of early Christian fellowship and witness. If Jesus was "the man for others," always giving himself to them so that he ran the risk of being identified with them—outsiders, sinners, Gentiles even—then our giving ourselves must not stop short of putting ourselves in peril. If Jesus, on occasion, put prayer above food, sleep, company, even "works of mercy" (Mark 1:32–39), where reflection before decision was necessary (the sorting-out of priorities, we would say), then, in a culture where everything is accelerated confusion, how much more it is demanded of us that we go aside, unseen, so that when we reappear we may have a sense of direction. If Jesus set aside humanly proper aims, claims, relationships ("keeping-up-with" friends, family, church, country) for something more urgent, are we not similarly to disencumber ourselves when the call reaches us? Perhaps until we do, from time to time, so "unload," we may not know there *is* a call.

The speed of changing, the complexity of choices open to us, the tendency to discard as soon as the first flush of interest is gone, all cry out for an underlying orientation. The old analogy of training, of disciplined practice, may still be useful. What is needed in athletics, languages, the arts or technology, in order to achieve the freedom of mastery, may be deepened to apply to the Christian way, the whole direction of life. The orientation runs deeper than a set "life-style." A great variety of styles (compounded of everything from hair to politics) may serve the Christian folk, because their "difference" is not to be observed in these observables (perhaps not necessarily even in a Sunday schedule) but in the key, the mode, the consistency of touch. It is not for people to say of Christians, "See how they give, how they worship, how they deny themselves," but rather, "Why are they able to bring to all things, to everyone they touch a new 'lift', a new openness, and a new—yes—kind of love?"

Our Religious Face
No Name-Tag

The First Sunday in Lent

Lutheran	*Roman Catholic*	*Episcopal*	*Pres./UCC/Chr.*	*Methodist/COCU*
Gen. 2:7-9, 15-17; 3:1-7	Gen. 2:7-9; 3:1-7	Gen. 2:7-9, 15-17; 3:1-7a	Gen. 2:7-9; 3:1-7	Gen. 2:7-9, 15-17; 3:1-7a
Rom. 5:12 (13-16), 17-19	Rom. 5:12-19	Rom. 5:12-19	Rom. 5:12-19	Rom. 5:12-19
Matt. 4:1-11	Matt. 4:1-11	Matt. 4:1-11	Matt. 4:1-11	Matt. 4:1-11

EXEGESIS

First Lesson: Gen. 2:7–9, 15–17; 3:1–7. The selection of these verses suggests that one concentrate upon the so-called Fall of Adam and Eve. Such isolation, however, is dangerous, since it implies an isolation of those passages which are heavily burdened with a long tradition of misinterpretation. To this tradition belongs the identification of the serpent with Satan, the understanding of the "fall" as the discovery of the sinful sexual dimension of human life, and the interpretation of the female as the origin of sinful desire. None of these traditional interpretations can claim to have any basis in this text. If one wants to avoid the pitfalls of the deeply rooted traditional interpretations, one must consider the total context from which these verses are taken, i.e., Gen. 2:4–3:24.

The author of these two chapters has welded together two older narratives which must have belonged to the religious tradition of storytelling from times immemorial. The first narrative is a creation story which underlies approximately Gen. 2:4–8 and 18–24. This story is deeply dissatisfied with the traditional view of creation: that man was created as a single human being out of clay and animated with the divine breath: "God said, 'It is not good . . .'" (2:18). Man and woman are social beings who support each other ("helper"). Only the two together in their mutual cooperation constitute mankind. This is finally expressed in the conclusion in 2:24. Although this, of course, includes the sexual relationship, it is by no means the primary motif in the story.

The second narrative used in Genesis 2–3 is of an entirely different character. The author prepares for it already in chap. 2 by the insertion of the description of paradise (2:9–17 and 25). The details which are given about paradise (its abundance and marvels and the tree of life) contrast with the statements concerning human existence in 3:16–19 (pain, toil, sweat and death). The question is: Why is paradise closed to human beings, and why is the life of human beings such a burdensome short episode? The answer is given in a form which demonstrates the highly developed art of the narrator (dramatic action and dialogue) as well as a high degree of sophistication. The story also employs a number of mythical concepts of Babylonian and Canaanite origin (the tree of life, the rivers of paradise, the figure of the serpent). Gen. 3:1–7 constitutes the center of the dramatic action and dialogue and explains why the cultural and economic situation of people is what it is, and why there is no possibility of a return into "paradise."

"To be like God and (because of that) to possess immortality" would be understood in the context of ancient oriental myth as the sharing of divine food which makes immortal. Such a narrative would normally be told about the jealousy of two gods, one who is protecting the secret of the tree that he possesses—thus the command not to eat from it—and another god who is trying to destroy such a scheme and to expose the jealous prohibition. Later Christian sects like the gnostic Ophites revived such myths; for them, the serpent was the representative of the true God who saves men from the jealous tyranny of the God of the OT.

In its biblical form the story has been deprived of its mythical implications. The serpent has become "just" a vicious animal (cf. 3:14–15), although the author seems fully aware of the religious symbolism of the serpent; but in degrading it into an animal the author closes the door to an understanding of "to be like God" in a religious sense. The man and the woman have indeed become like God by eating from the tree (cf. 3:22!), but in a different sense: they have attained "knowledge of good and evil." This knowledge has no special relationship to sexual desire, and that it is the woman who eats first has no material significance for the meaning of the story (rather it is a part of the highly developed art of the narrator). Nor is "good and evil" meant in a moral sense; it is a cultural rather than a moral concept, i.e., "good" implies such notions as "useful," "profitable," "helpful." As God's "goodness" is the ability to invent and to create, the corresponding knowledge of human beings is the wisdom and inventiveness that creates culture and civilization. Thus the author emphasizes the cultural progress from nakedness (2:25) to garments from plants (3:7) and finally to garments from animal skins (3:21)—a realistic assessment of man's situation in the cultural world outside of paradise which speaks against the suggestion of religious myth that reaches out for immortality.

However, the understanding of that post-paradise cultural situation is by no means secular. On the contrary, a trespass of divine law caused this situation, and a divine curse determines its conditions. That is the price paid for cultural progress: not immediate death, but toil and hardship and eventual death. To this theological view of human life and culture corresponds a deeply religious view of the "original sin." It was not simply the transgression of some kind of prohibition, but it was an action through which these human beings together wanted to obtain divine status for themselves, to become masters of their own affairs. This original sin is confronted with the only realistic consequence: human life under the curse (3:14–19) and a paradise that is definitely closed (3:24).

Second Lesson: Rom. 5:12 (13–16), 17–19. Rom. 5:12–21 speaks of the situation of all human beings under the rule of sin and death. It reflects Jewish and gnostic mythical speculations about the primordial man and the heavenly redeemer which played a significant role in Paul's time (cf. also 1 Cor. 15:21–22, 45–49). Such speculations imply a fateful identity with a primordial figure and understand condemnation and salvation in terms of an inescapable participation. As Paul delineates his typology of Adam and Christ, he repeatedly implies criticisms of such concepts and their consequences. This is the primary reason for the complex sentence structure of this difficult passage. Paul uses the typology, but he wants to avoid its logical conclusions, since he sees the salvation through Christ as an order of existence that allows neither strict correspondence to the old order of Adam nor a relation of fateful necessity.

Rom. 5:12 begins with a citation of a current Jewish understanding of the 2nd and 3rd chapter of the Book of Genesis: through one single man (Adam) and his transgression death came into the world. Paul inserts "sin came into the world." It is not just death that all humans have to suffer because of Adam's transgression (perhaps even innocently), but all are involved—"because all have sinned." Since Augustine this sentence has been read "in him (i.e. Adam) all have sinned" and such reading was used to argue for a doctrine of original sin, an inescapable fate into which everybody was born as a child of Adam. But even though Paul says that sin is an all-encompassing reality, the correct reading of the last phrase of v. 12 leaves no doubt that it is everyone's active participation which makes the total Adamic mankind subject to both sin and death.

The expected corresponding phrase "thus life came to all through Christ's obedience" does not occur. Instead, 5:13 begins two parentheses. The first, 5:13–14, makes clear that the involvement in sin is not limited to the situation in which sin can be "counted" by means of the law. This underlines the universality of sin. If questioned, Paul might have argued, as he did in Rom. 1:18 ff, that the will of God was known to everyone from the beginning of creation (cf. also Rom. 7:8 ff: the law only makes one consciously aware of sin). The concluding line of 5:14

introduces the theme of the second parenthesis: "Adam, who was a type of the one to come." The following typology, however, breaks the correspondence of Adam and Christ already in its external structure. The formulation in 5:15 and 5:16–17 emphasizes that there is no analogy: ". . . not like . . . , [but] much more . . ." The typologies become antitheses. The first of these (5:15) says that they are incomparable, because what God has freely given (cf. the repetition of the terms "free gift" and "grace") belongs to an entirely different dimension of reality than the transgression of Adam. Salvation cannot be understood as a simple return to Adam's original status of bliss—such is the tenor of many Jewish and gnostic interpretations of the first chapters of Genesis. The second antithesis (5:16a) is followed by two explanations (5:16b and 5:17) which depart even more radically from the structure of a typology. It is no longer a question of Adam and Christ corresponding to each other, but Adam's trespass is set in juxtaposition to the trespasses of the many: "One trespass brought condemnation—the many trespasses bring justification" (5:16b). Similarly in the second explanation: "Through Adam's trespass death reigned—through Christ those who receive the abundance of grace will reign" (5:17).

Grace and life are not the simple opposites of sin and death. Sin is indeed a fateful power. Grace, however, establishes its richness on the basis of the abundance of trespasses, using its opposite for its own purposes. The Adamic mankind is caught in a closed circle of sin and death in which tyranny and slavery are the structure of existence. Grace, however, reaches right into that vicious circle and puts those who accept it on a path which will lead them to the possession of life and kingship. This calls for different imagery; there is no such thing as a closed circle of grace and life. Rather, there is a paradoxical relationship of past, present, and future. The past, determined by trespasses, establishes the "rule of grace" (Rom. 5:21); the future of life and kingship is already anticipated in the freedom and the righteousness of the present in spite of the tribulations (Rom. 5:3 f).

With these qualifications Paul can return to the sentence which he began in 5:12, but had left incomplete. Rom. 5:18 and 19 bring two typological theses in strict parallelism. But the correspondence intended by the initial sentence in 5:12—death for all through Adam's disobedience, life for all through Christ's obedience—does not occur. Instead, 5:18 juxtaposes condemnation with acquittal; 5:19 contrasts "to be made sinners" with "to be made righteous." The primary usefulness of the Adam-typology was that it provided Paul with an opportunity to emphasize the universality of salvation, since it spoke of the universality of condemnation. But when the new situation of the believers is characterized as "righteousness," it is a conscious move from a fateful past into an historical dimension of faith, i.e., an existence that takes account of its past and that understands the present as the realization of a final fulfillment which is yet to come.

Gospel: Matt. 4:1–11. The story of Jesus' temptation in the Gospels of Matthew and Luke is derived from the second common source of these two Gospels, the synoptic sayings source ("Q"). It replaces the briefer account of Mark 1:12–13 which presents Jesus as the man in paradise; cf. the contemporary Jewish Testament of Naphtali 8:4: "Both men and angels shall bless you, . . . and the devil shall flee from you, and the wild beasts shall fear you." The mention of the 40 days in the wilderness belongs to this motif. Israel was in the wilderness for 40 years; Moses spent 40 days on the holy mountain (Exod. 34:28); Elijah was on the mountain of God for 40 days (I Kings 19:8). Thus the temptation of Jesus was originally seen as the initiation of the return into paradise.

In the source of Matthew and Luke, the story has been expanded into a Haggadah, i.e., an interpretation of the law for edification and admonition in the form of a narrative (to be distinguished from the Halakah which is an interpretation of the law in the form of rules for conduct). This excludes three rather widespread interpretations of our text: (1) The historicizing understanding which sees in this text a report of Jesus' temptation to become a political Messiah. (2) The psychological interpretation which speaks about the struggle of Jesus with respect to the question whether or not he should assume the exercise of divine power. (3) The dogmatic theologian's interest that wants to use this narrative as evidence that Jesus subordinated his own actions under God's will. As a Haggadah, this story speaks about those temptations which are a threat to every faithful Christian. Thus, this text is concerned with a problem of conduct and ethics. This ethical problem, for the early church, was the problem of the miracle and its justification. In more modern terms we might say it is the question of the demonstration of divine power versus the acceptance of God's will.

The first temptation uses the stay in the wilderness as a narrative motive to motivate the tempter's question: Why not make bread out of stone, if you are hungry? It implies that not only Jesus, but also the Christian who possesses the Spirit can accomplish such a miracle. The answer, quoting Deut. 8:3, refuses the exercise of such power, since it is God's business to perform a miracle when it is needed. It is more important to trust God than to demonstrate the power of the Spirit. Christians have no obligation whatsoever to save the world through their wonderful accomplishments.

The second temptation changes the scene. The devil himself becomes the leader. It is exactly the trust in God which Jesus had emphasized in the answer to the first temptation that is now expressed in the scriptural quotation (Ps. 91:11–12) used by the devil! One should not ascribe this to the ingenuity of the devil; the early Christians knew that Scripture could be used against them. According to the principle already used in Judaism that one scriptural passage criticizes the other, the Book of Deuteronomy (6:16) again provides the answer: he who asks for a miracle makes experiments with God. If Christians do that, they are not demonstrating their trust in God, but they are frivolously creating situations which do not leave any other choices to God than to perform a miracle.

A new scene is also chosen for the third temptation. There is an obvious difference, if one compares this one to the first and second temptations, since now the devil drops any pretense of piety: "Worship me!" One misses the point of this scene if one understands it to mean that everyone who is after the good things of this world (power, a good life, comfort, etc.) will ultimately fall under the power of the devil. Rather, the worship of Satan is the beginning and the condition of the possession of the world. What is at stake is the opposition of mutually exclusive claims of power. This is made clear by Jesus' answer which quotes the confession of faith of Jews and Christians that there is only one God whom one must worship (Deut. 6:13).

The church has to recognize that its own situation is still one before the final fulfillment. The temptations of Jesus are exemplary for the continuing situation of the church. Matt. 4:1–11 is a question to the church, whether it will be able to make realistic and loyal decisions in situations in which the devil is as powerful as ever in his ability to seduce Christians on the basis of scriptural beliefs, or even openly, into his service.

HOMILETICAL INTERPRETATION

Notice how humanness runs through these readings: what it is to be human, how to stay human, what is the inherent danger of humanness, is there more than one way to be human? Underlying is the crucial question of power and allegiance, and, therefore, the meaning and use of human power(s). Sex is one such power, but only obsession makes it the sole clue (see exegesis of Genesis 2) and we must neither be obsessed with it nor ignore it. How relate it all to Lent?

Note the popular misconceptions against which we have to work (see exegesis), especially in the Genesis passages. These cannot be overcome in one sermon and we need not "turn people off" by using the word "myth"; it is what myth does that we need to talk about in less upsetting terms. A myth explores the more-than-obvious dimensions of the human problem. It is best to get at something basic and keep the congregation's mind on it by opening up the theme in all the lessons at once.

Fundamentally, two kinds of humanness are at stake—primordial and eschatological (but not those words, please). In the old story of origins Adam disobeys when he is offered the chance to be as a god himself (rejecting his humanness), unaware that he will thereby submit himself to a new allegiance. The result is the human condition of "blood, toil, tears and sweat." Paradise is closed, no longer an option, people cannot go back to it. (This we learn beyond the Lesson.) So whatever is to be sought is to be found by looking ahead (eschatology) not by reversion.

Is then humanness a disaster? As Paul says, we are stuck with it (because of "Adam"— nothing to do with original sin brought on by the discovery of copulation!). But you cannot go back and be Adam before his ill-fated decision. We have to look elsewhere than Rousseau's "noble savage." It is not *just* kings and priests, institutions and the "establishment," that keep us from enjoying our humanity. We cannot "cop out" or be "drop-outs." What we need and what we have is a new vision of humanity (new "Adam"), when, by a deliberate choice, Adam's choice is rejected and another made.

There are two extremes, both wide of the mark. One gives up. There is a beast in us, it argues, so we cannot be blamed if we act as beasts—whether sexually, or by the use of power. To picture the beast as naturally violent and death-dealing, even against his own species, is a libel on the animal kingdom. The other extreme tries to escape from humanness by human means; humanity is supreme, so it can use anything, including itself, and still come out ahead. "Back to square one." Both beast and create-your-own-destiny are forms of allegiance—or misalliance.

That is what Matthew makes clear. It is all too easy to be less than human, easiest of all to treat others as less than human. To try to be more than human is to end by being less than human. The destiny of humans is not to be other than human—we had best grasp that. The profound truth of the incarnation is that God became human to save humanness, to make it after the pattern of Christ's humanity, and not to transform us into angels or anything else. If we were not intended to be beasts, neither were we designed to become cherubs or seraphs nor, in all seriousness, robots.

When obedience fails, what then? We are dependent on knowledge (Adam's discovery). That is, we are confined to human philosophy, sciences, and technics and this, curiously (or by providence), could turn out to make us less than human. We, as humans, stand dangerously near the point where our control over nature, the biosphere or the environment, including our own environment of the body and mind, could tempt us to take it all into our own hands, even the powers that have hitherto operated through heredity, and make both earth and humankind after our own likeness. At that point we may already have crossed the threshold to destruction. We have glimpsed how fragile the "spaceship earth" is for the support of technological, power-crazed humanity, and the human personality may not be too resistant to becoming a computer.

To take our destiny into our own hands, holding no allegiance, no responsibility to anyone else, does not mean freedom but only putting ourselves under another control. We may call it (mythically) "the Devil," or may wisely prefer "Satan," that is, translated, "the Adversary." In this way we are referring to anything inimical to humanness as revealed in Christ (mythically "the second Adam"). Participation in one or the other is "inescapable" (Koester) and there has to be a decision, a commitment, substantiated by myriad choices to follow. The antitheses, so easily formulated in theology or explained in the pulpit, are an eerie conglomerate, a murky mix at the points where their ends are hidden, and they wear masks to conceal their real features. The whole question of the issues of humanness and the divine intention is open-ended. That is, open at the forward-looking end. We cannot, after all, go back and be Adam with no apple to tempt him, or Adam with no Eve (see the exegesis).

This is one way of dealing with the temptation narratives. Undoubtedly Jesus is not here thought of as reversing the failure of Adam under temptation so much as the testing of Israel in the wilderness. In the case of Adam, of Israel, and of Jesus alike, the *test* ("temptation" having been degraded in modern usage) was not a simple one, but basically, whatever the form (tree of life, manna from heaven, stones into bread), the question whether God could be made to give proof, justify himself to people, put into any one man's hands the ability to prove beyond any doubt that he or any one of them was acting for God himself. The test of being able to resist or not resist the taking of power into human hands and claiming it to be God's intention is the real test. The issue is always obedience—in the sense of allegiance shown by participation. To participate in the "power-game" is to follow another leader, to submit to another rule by the very claim to be free.

There is nothing whatever archaic about the issues connected with the temptation, nor are they purely moral in the limited sense of a private ethic. The issues have one factor basic to the human situation—the use of power for control of people, especially the temptation to ascribe *successful* power uses to God even when used against his ultimate and fundamental interest. The devil is that "other," that adversary whose inevitable gimmick from time immemorial has been to commend power, even to offer power, in order to enslave the power-wielder by leading him to think God owes him its use.

We can, in effect, almost literally turn stones into bread. But the point is that "bread" is a form of power, "bread" in its broadest sense of all the basics of human sustenance, human energy, human delight. It has always been used as a means of control, either through manipulation of its production or distribution, now on a world-wide scale. Anyone who could guarantee it and the energy it released could have control. So Jesus is challenged to settle for that as the proof that God is indeed his Father. And Jesus' response is, "That is not all there is to it." Man lives, "not by bread alone," but by ultimate understanding and allegiance. Whether bread is a divine gift depends upon whether it is used to enslave people or to set them free, to deprive them of their essential humanity or to make them truly human.

Now (see the exegesis) "that other one" takes over the script and quotes the author of it, and finally comes out into the open to claim that he is able to provide better than God and hence can demand worship.

The working of wonders is a potent source of influence and control. Why not challenge God to make it available to the utmost, forcing God to give a clear sign and removing all doubts? Why not, indeed, since there seems to be clear Scripture for it. People can become *addicted* to marvels. They find themselves dependent on circuses as well as on bread. But it is like all other forms of addiction, self-defeating. One needs bigger and better wonders; one is willing to barter freedom for the more powerful stuff. That means slavery to the provider.

It bothered the early Christians that Jesus' works of power had not been conclusive, as his opponents are said to have pointed out to the very end. The place where a sign is demanded that will resolve all doubt is the temple, but Jesus has been led there, not by the Spirit, but by that other. And, as Luther was advised to reflect, and as Paul demanded, the spirits must be tested, for undoubted wonders are not self-authenticating. In whose allegiance and to what end are they performed? Exorcism is clearly a means of setting free, and so is physical healing, but the church is not solely a physical therapy center. There is also a freedom to be attained when the illness is not removed. God, Jesus answered, is not to be put to the test. You cannot resolve all doubts, give conclusive proof, and still leave man free.

The issue of political control, enforced militarily or economically or by any other use of power, is possible, fatally possible as we have learned. But what does its full exercise involve, or what does full submission indicate? Both "the other one" and Jesus are shown to know the answer. Worship. Nothing less. Something more ultimate than submission, the final form of obedience which is surrender of body, mind, and spirit. The price—to sacrifice humanness at its vital point of freedom.

It is clear that three things are rejected. Nothing is said about the outcome. If none of these three roads, then what? How can the kingdom be established? The evangelists give no immediate answer. In other words, the issue is "open-ended."

Sadly, we have not found in the human situation other means of imposing order on human confusion than by these three general means that Jesus is depicted as rejecting. We seldom seem to reach for any others. What then? The open end, Paul says, is Jesus himself—a new humanness. Not Adam repeated, but Adam reversed, his situation not simply retrieved, but man new and of "different dimensions" with no "closed circle." As different, really, as worship in its fullest sense (which we have yet to experience) is from obedience. Jesus, in the Gospel images, rejects participation with "the other," seeing it as utterly alien, unthinkable, the ultimate denial of true worship. The Christ-Adam is not primordial man refurbished, but the eschatological Lord. Humanness is caught up in Christ, a new prospect, undefinable in detail until we achieve the willingness to accept it as a gift from God.

The question then is, can we live without a final answer, that is, live by anticipation? The biblical answer, the NT one in a special sense, is yes. It is anticipation based on recital of the past indicators (*anamnesis* is the liturgical term, but don't use it!), an entering into the past which is more than recital. Not return to the past, but a present encounter with it at the point where it is met by the impact of what is to come, and so transformed. The Christian lives where the past and the future (*eschaton*) meet. The recollections become anticipation, and there the sacraments operate. The human situation is not to be done away with, its history discarded, the characteristic of humanness abandoned. We are to be new people, but people; human still, free at last to find being so no longer a burden but a triumph, because we have given ourselves to Christ and there is our life, our shape, our stature, our destiny.

The Second Sunday in Lent

Lutheran	*Roman Catholic*	*Episcopal*	*Pres./UCC/Chr.*	*Methodist/COCU*
Gen. 12:1-8	Gen. 12:1-4a	Gen. 12:1-8	Gen. 12:1-7	Gen. 12:1-8
Rom. 4:1-5, 13-17	2 Tim. 1:8b-10	Rom. 5:1-10	2 Tim. 1:8-14	Rom. 4:1-5, 13-17
John 4:5-26	Matt. 17:1-9	John 4:5-26	Matt. 17:1-9	John 4:5-26

EXEGESIS

First Lesson: Gen. 12:1–8. Chaps. 11 and 12 mark the rather abrupt transition from the story of all humankind (Gen. 1–11) to the story of a single human family (Gen. 12–50)—and yet it is this single family which receives a promise that has worldwide significance (Gen. 12:3). Gen. 11:1–9 concludes the story of all human races by telling of the disaster that followed upon the building of the tower of Babel. The following narratives about Abraham, Isaac, and Jacob are dominated by the two promises of the land and of a multitude of offspring (cf. Gen. 12:3, 7; 13:14–16; 15:3, 7, 18; etc.). Both promises remain strangely suspended throughout the book of Genesis. Because of the experiences caused by such delay, the focus changes from God's acting with all peoples to the problems of individuals which are not without many trivial and romantic details. In the Abraham stories the primary factor is the delay of the offspring, brought to a climax when Abraham is requested to sacrifice his son who has finally arrived—against all expectations (Gen. 22). Since God's behavior is presented as extremely trying and frustrating, the central problem of the Abraham narratives becomes "faith" (cf. Gen. 15:6). This problem of Abraham's faith is nowhere solved by references to the law (there is no ritual law, nor priests, etc.). Only after the exile and primarily in the wisdom literature (cf. also Philo of Alexandria, the contemporary of Jesus who wrote two treatises on Abraham) does Abraham become the primary example of religious virtue in his fulfillment of the law, and thus a "friend of God."

Gen. 12:1–8 was written by the first literary editor of the Abraham narratives after they had been told orally for many centuries. The divine command to Abraham is formulated in such a way that the whole literary context is in view; detailed geographical information reveals that its author was a man of learning and wisdom. There is a detailed description of the secure social situation which Abraham has to leave (Gen. 12:1), but no indication of the religious situation in which

Abraham was—a factor which plays no role whatever in the Abraham stories! In contrast to the present security of Abraham the statement about the land of the future remains vague, and the promise that he will become a great nation appears as quite unbelievable (Gen. 11:30 had stated that Sarai was barren). The "blessing" (12:2–3) includes the well-being in the total realm of life; 12:3 expands it to all humankind. (Note the contrast to Gen. 11:1–9.) The deliberate sending out of one single family into an uncertain land with uncertain offspring is the all-inclusive act of God by which the blessing is to be extended to all peoples.

Haran is the place that Abraham leaves (12:4). It was actually a city, but is not presented as such—perhaps the picture of the nomadic origin of the fathers is still visible here. Canaan (12:5) means the whole area of the land west of the Jordan, including Phoenicia, more specifically Palestine. Even though this whole land was promised to Abraham as his possession, 12:6–9 still presents Abraham as a nomadic foreigner. He settles briefly in the central part, at Shechem and near Bethel (both places later become important sanctuaries in Israel's history), then in the Negeb, south of Judea. Gen. 12:10–19 finds Abraham in Egypt. These notices contain traditions and memories of the migrations of Semite people into the lands of the fertile crescent during the second millennium B.C., partly substantiated through excavations and through information from other sources. They also retain the self-consciousness of migrating people who do not derive their dignity from other established cultures. What begins here has the freshness of adventure, not only theologically, but also sociologically and culturally. But all this remains secondary to the great theme: It is the Lord God who sends Abraham on his way; and Abraham not only obeys—he has no other thought than to build an altar to this God wherever he goes. Thus, this introduction to the Abraham stories places Abraham's faith in the divine command squarely into the realities of historical developments, and it makes no effort to reconcile the improbabilities of the fulfillment of the promise with them.

Second Lesson: Rom. 4:1–5, 13–17. The theme for chap. 4 of the Epistle to the Romans is given in 3:27–31. "Boasting" (3:27) is the sum total of all of man's achievements, religious, moral, and otherwise. It cannot be excluded by the "law," since the law seeks to be fulfilled through works, and when that happens, boasting is inevitable. The term "law" in Paul means any kind of law that invites "works," i.e., fulfillment by doing, not only the law of Moses. On the other hand, when Paul says, "we uphold the law," (3:31) he means specifically the law of the OT which is the expression of the will of God. That "law," however, does not invite works, it calls for faith.

Rom. 4:1–25 gives the scriptural proof for Paul's thesis of "justification by faith" (cf. Rom. 3:21–26). But there are also elements which belong to the style of a Greek diatribe (cf. the rhetorical questions in 4:1 and 10; see also the same diatribe style in 3:27–31). The subject matter invites polemical discourse and paradoxical formulations. There are three parts: (1) Abraham's justification by faith, 4:1–8; (2) its validity for circumcised and uncircumcised, 4:9–12; (3) the promise of Abraham, 4:13–25. The Second Lesson for this Sunday treats the beginning of the first and of the third part.

The first rhetorical question (4:1) already denies the right of all current interpretations of the figure of Abraham. Their purpose was to show that Abraham was obedient and therefore called a friend of God (in the NT cf. James 2:21–23). Paul asks: "What then, shall we say, has Abraham, our father according to the flesh, found?" (this translation, which differs from the RSV, is supported by most ancient witnesses). The answer is "grace;" cf. Gen. 18:3: "If I have found grace (RSV translates "favor") in your sight." If Abraham had found recognition for his obedience, he had something to boast about. But if he found grace, there was no reason for boasting—which would be impossible before God anyway; thus, he was not justified by works (cf. 3:27). Rom. 4:3 quotes Gen. 15:6 and introduces a term, translated by "to reckon" in the RSV, and repeatedly used here. It comes from the language of business and means "to book to someone's account" (as credit or debt). Rom. 4:4 quotes a general rule which points to the absurdity of introducing the notion of "grace" into the world of business where work and wages should correspond to each other. On the other hand, the kind of "accounting" which God does, also does not fit the world of religious values. This is shown by 4:5, the most important sentence in this passage. In one of the writings of the sect from the Dead Sea it is seen as one of the worst examples of godlessness "to declare the ungodly righteous" (CD 1:19)—as distinct from accepting the repentant sinner which is, of course, a pious act. Paul states, however, that God "justified the ungodly." The term "ungodly" is the extreme opposite of "pious" and "religious." For Paul, Abraham is the example of faith in that God who justifies the impious and irreligious.

Rom. 4:6–8 adds another scriptural witness, Ps. 32:1–2, because God is also seen in this passage as the one who does not "reckon" sin. Rom. 4:9–12 returns to Abraham, this time to Gen. 17:10–11, in order to discuss a second point: the significance of Abraham's faith for the history of salvation. In 4:13–17, "promise" is the decisive term. It is not the promise relating to the future in general, but specifically the word of God as given to the fathers (cf. Rom. 15:8; Abraham in Rom. 4 and Gal. 3; Isaac in Gal. 4). For the Jew, this promise is closely related to the law; fulfillment of law and covenant puts the promise into operation. For Paul, there is no connection between promise and law, because the promise to Abraham entails the inheritance of the whole world. Thus 4:13 speaks against the particularistic limitations of the promise. Rom. 4:14 parallels promise and faith, and it denies the connection between inheritance and law, since any law produces transgression—a problem which cannot be solved within the realm of the "law" (4:15). "Faith," however, signifies a realm in which God is free to act and to grant ("grace") whatever he wishes. Only then can God's action be guaranteed to *all* people (cf. the repetition of this word in 4:16). The quotation of Gen. 17:5 in Rom. 4:17 serves as confirmation of this thesis. God is not satisfied with giving good (or bad) grades to pious and moral people. Justification by law is the godlessness of people who have something to boast about—an insult to God's power and freedom. God is the creator who, through his sovereign power, calls things into being out of nothing, gives life to the dead. "Faith" is the reliance upon the God who has already begun his new creation through the raising of Jesus from the dead (4:24–25)—not something which *we* can "reckon" in a neat schema of sin and forgiveness: *God* "reckons." Christian accounts of reckoning are no better than those of other people. Abraham becomes a witness against us, because he found nothing—except grace.

Gospel: John 4:5–26. These verses are a section from the chapter "Jesus and the Samaritan Woman" (John 4:1–42) which the author of the Gospel composed on the basis of a tradition that was written in order to justify the Christian mission to the Samaritans. There was resistance in the early church against such missionary work (Matt. 10:5), but Acts 8:1, 5 reports that it began at a very early date. The story used in John 4 (comprising approximately 4:5–9, 16–19, and parts of 20–26, 31–42) told of the acceptance of the Christian message by a Samaritan town and preserved the memory of a woman as the founder of the church. The author of the Gospel has utilized this traditional story in order to clarify two problems, the relationship of Christian faith to traditional religious beliefs, and the relationship of the witnesses and their message to the person of Jesus. The discussion of the first problem comprises vv. 5–26. The text is best divided into three parts: (1) exposition of the situation, 4:5–9; (2) preparation of the revelation, 4:10–20; (3) self-revelation of Jesus, 4:21–26.

The exposition of the story reveals knowledge of the locality (the town of Sychar is not mentioned in the OT). Jesus was tired (4:6)—a frequent motif in such narratives; the mention of the sixth hour (= noon) motivates the following request for some refreshing water. Question and answer in 4:9 state the problem: because of the Samaritan schism, no such fellowship is possible. Or, in terms of the interests of the traditional story: Is it legitimate that the (Jewish-)Christian mission carries the Gospel to the schismatic Samaritans?

John 4:10 begins a discourse with a question of Jesus that creates the misunderstanding which is so typical for the Gospel of John. It lifts the discussion to a different level: not "Jews and Samaritans" is the problem, but "living water." The question of the Christian revelation makes the important religious controversy between Jews and Samaritans irrelevant. "Living water" is, on the one hand, the normal oriental term for "fresh water;" it is, on the other hand, the "water of life" (cf. the bread of life, John 6), i.e., the water from heaven that gives eternal life. This double meaning gives rise to the misunderstanding (4:11–12). Jesus' identification of the water that he can give (4:13–14) causes yet another misunderstanding: the woman thinks of magic water that will renew itself continuously (4:15). Only the disclosure of the truth about herself (4:16–18) results in her recognition that Jesus is neither an ordinary man, nor a magician; as a "prophet" he lays open the confusion of her own personal life (4:19).

If he is a prophet, Jesus should also be able to address himself to the religious and political confusion of Israel, i.e., the schism between Jews and Samaritans symbolized in the two different places of worship (4:20). Jesus' answer confronts this alternative with the eschatological worship "in spirit and in truth" which does not know any particular holy places that could give legitimacy to cult and prayer (cf. also Rev. 21:22: there is no temple in the new Jerusalem). No doubt, this eschatological time has come and is already present (4:21–22). V. 22 disturbs this eschatological statement of revelation; the statement that salvation comes from the Jews is either a later gloss or an ironic remark. "Spirit" and "truth" are terms which designate the eschatological coming of God; "spirit" is his power which creates a new life (cf. 3:5–8). There is no thought of a "spiritualized" concept of prayer and worship; "truth" is the reality of the new existence (cf. 3:21; 16:13). The woman understands that Jesus is speaking about the eschatological renewal of everything "when the Messiah comes" (4:25). But she does not understand the "now." Jesus' self-revelation (4:26) not only discloses the "now" of the fulfillment of the expectation, it also changes the situation radically. It is no longer a debate that maintains a certain detachment, but it is an event which requires response and action. The only thing that matters now is the new message (4:29).

HOMILETICAL INTERPRETATION

First Lesson. The Abraham we read of here is the Father. He is the father of the Hebrews, of the Jewish people. He is the father of faith, of all those who will believe in God in Abraham's way of believing. He is the father of those who worship everywhere, the universal church.

When we meet him he is all this proleptically, potentially, in possibility only, not in immediate fact. His secure confidence in the God who calls is, in the end, proof against doubts, scorn, hazards, and tests. Sometimes he is compelled to believe in spite of the evidence. At times he tries to take matters into his own hands, to conduct transactions, even with the Lord. But his basic, unassailable confidence in God leaves the future open.

We sometimes preach as though faith solves all problems, on the spot; as though the saints were perfect, at every moment. The Bible gives this no support. Life is confusing, and even the saints are confused. Moreover, things do not make sense, neither do people (especially people), on the surface. It is on a deeper level, but a more determinative level, it is in the long view, at a more conclusive end, that the transformation of faith is found.

Abraham starts with a turning away, a departure, and a journey. Security behind him, he now has no road map, no pre-announced destination. That is in the mind of God. On God's ultimate disclosure Abraham is dependent and this must suffice to explain the day-to-day obscurities. No "flight-plan," no itinerary, no routing, but in place of it—God; God present, God reiterating his word, God putting Abraham to the test (read the other stories of Abraham; it is all there). "Leave." "Go." "I will show you."

First, Abraham commits everything. He burns his bridges behind him. He cannot go back (see last Sunday). He can go only forward. But ahead lies not only "the land I will show you" but also the universal significance in his doings for all the peoples of the earth. In a sense the first three verses are the text for the whole of the Bible that follows.

So how does it work out? At the start Abraham goes from place to place. It is as if he had read, "Do not be anxious about tomorrow; tomorrow will be anxious for itself. Let the day's troubles be sufficient for today." Sometimes what we have to do, and not only in illness, is to get through the next hour, the present day, so that we may come to the next with an open road still before us. How? By confidence that God is one step ahead (at least) and will meet us when we get there.

So next, at each stopping-place, Abraham sets up an altar to his God. It is a means of affirming his contact, his recognition that God is around —even in this strange place. But the altar is set up also as a marker, a testimony or witness. His route becomes dotted with altars that are way-signs for those who come after, affirmations that so far one is on the right track. Yet, if we want to trace a line through the woods we need more than one marker *behind us.* Two will enable us to get the direction through the brush where, as yet, we cannot see the final marker. Sometimes (v. 7) the Lord appears and confirms his intention. Sometimes (v. 8) he does not. But in any case Abraham calls on God's "Name," that is, God's revealed nature in this project, this connection. In this manner Abraham is able to journey on.

So, thank God, are we able to keep going. The basic orientation involves the underlying confidence that "God is as good as his word," meaning God's word is as good as he is. The ground of faith is that there is a destination and God has it in view even if we cannot see even the next step and can only take our sights from the points behind where we set up markers of faith. It involves the fundamental trust that God has, indeed, a "Name," that he is consistent with himself, he has a "nature." His nature will be, in all its disclosures, if infinitely richer and more complex, yet not different in essence; new, but not strange. That is "faith," Abraham's kind of faith, the Bible's faith, the faith (may we say?) of Jesus.

Second Lesson. But that is only the start. There are two stages, yet each is inherent in the Abraham of Genesis. Paul understands Abraham plotting the path to fulfillment, and the Christ of the Fourth Gospel speaks as the new Abraham entering into the fulfillment.

The only "rightness" Abraham had was God's direction, intention, presence. He appropriated it by the assurance that God was God! Faith alone we say, because it is grace alone and always, all the way along, since grace *was* the way. Abraham "blazed the trail," behind him. That is the only way a trail can be blazed. His getting where he was going was a reward, but not for laying out a route, or covering the ground, or beating down the obstacles, or any other achievement, but only because he had believed there would be both destination and reward and that they would be one and the same thing. (Would it help if we did not use the term "works" but, for a while at least, dealt in images? Nor "faith" until we give it some content, some active metaphor?)

In what sense can this image of a journey point to a God "who gives life to the dead" and "calls into existence things that do not exist?" In the sense that there was no "Oregon Trail" for the covered wagons to follow before the pioneers discovered that there *was* a way through the Rocky Mountains (in fact discovered that there were such mountains to be traversed). What Abraham had not seen, yet did see, what had not existed for him, yet was to be familiar, even home, had been "fore-seen," destined in advance to have reality, by God. That is part of the meaning of "God." The Abraham who arrived was "dead" before he arrived but, having arrived, lives as "Abraham-there." Abraham the Father is also Abraham the Founder (see exegesis).

This is life-in-faith, not in any banal "all will be well" manner, but in the Christian sense of living, living proleptically. For faith, in Abraham's sense, is "eschatological," the anticipation of what is already on its way to meet us. Faith is to operate in this way, expectant, so that it merges always into hope. For us to function in this way is to be "right" with God. Not that we are spectacular for our conviction, our efficiency, our achievement, our virtue. Far from it. We may hesitate, query, and be querulous, try to transact instead of trust, not apparently achieve anything, least of all holiness. Yet God is, in a sense, "queer." By our standards he is odd—simply because he regards us and treats us as we are to be, as though we had already arrived.

So the universality becomes possible, the "for all the peoples" which Abraham was promised. Not his genes but his genius (as a man of faith in this sense) gives birth to descendants, to a universal folk. No set of rules set up for a circumscribed group but faith-action marks the inheritors of the promise. There can be no limits to this response to a God on whom to impose limits would be to make him at once "not-God." Only on this basis is there inheritance, is there any promise fulfilled. All this is prior to regulations, to "law" which can only regulate what has been and can never create what-is-not-yet. Nor is it determined by location. Later generations would make Abraham's "markers," his altars of recognition, into shrines, with established law, established hierarchies—in short, "establishment." But there is no "here" or "there" any more than there is a "this is he," or "that is he" (see Mark 13:21). Which brings us to Jesus and the woman.

Gospel. It is strange to think there was a time when the mission to non-Jews needed to be justified and explained. But it was so. By what right were Samaritans to be considered Christians? The Jewish synagogue no doubt attacked the church for this liberality and put them outside the Jewish pale (and maybe even some Christians did the same), as illegitimate children of Abraham. We even get a glimpse of a new kind of universality, one with no distinction of sex any more than of nation, race, or of culture (see Gal. 3:28, so long in effect ignored by the churches and by "Christian" societies).

Here again is our theme of local shrines. The schism of locality, as well as schisms of culture (even of accent), of region, of color, of class, of "net worth," are far from unknown to Christianity even now. Full fellowship is thereby excluded, even extending to the sacraments, though they are still designated "sacraments of *grace*."

When we live on these levels we cannot *hear* the word of God. We do not "listen" to Jesus, much less "see" him. The author of John (see exegesis) uses the device of a remark of Jesus understood on one level to provide the cue for raising it to another level. In this chapter, a well that runs dry, to be cleared or re-dug, raised to an ever-flowing spring which has its source in no earthly location. Only the divine transcendence (as accepting-grace transcends boasting-effort) can bring people to rise above inherited or acquired presuppositions. Not only the woman wanted to fit Jesus into her previous categories, but so do we. We make Jesus a "guru" or a "superstar" or a guarantor of success—each can name his own category. A localized Jesus, a captured, tagged, and filed-away Jesus cannot bring the kind of release suggested by the access to living water.

We do that kind of "localizing" precisely to keep Jesus from disturbing us. Yet in the Gospels he is an "offence" (see John 7:43; 9:16; 10:19). A non-disturbing Jesus has no relation to the Christ of God or even to the Jesus of the Gospels. When the woman found that in his presence she was able to face her own situation, even to talk about it to others (for the first time?) she had discovered a new kind of freedom, a freedom which would not exhaust itself in ennui or satiation as so many of our fads do.

The legitimizing of worship (its "validity") has taken up too much of the time and attention of churchpeople. It is legitimized (if that term is appropriate at all) by its end-results in the sense that it must always be "open-ended." We are only anticipating, as the "new wine" of the Kingdom is anticipated by the eucharistic wine, the Messianic bread only anticipated in daily bread, the destination only anticipated by our arrival at "way-stations." We tend to close the line at each depot, thinking, "This is it." Yet all journey metaphors have this (mundane) limitation. We move to *our* destination. God's designated destination for us moves towards *us*. It is not in this place or that, not this liturgy or the other, but in Christ, that we meet God. And meeting God means being met by God, which is not only the true mode of worship but its end and its beginning, its functioning and its goal.

We cannot, like the woman, dismiss such questions on the ground that the "Messiah" has not yet come. We cannot refuse to act because we cannot act perfectly. It is perhaps a peculiarly American delusion (or a Western one?) that all problems must have solutions. Can we solve God? Can the woman say, "I see it all now; this is the place because this is where I have had *my* revelation"? The answer: "Neither in this place nor in Jerusalem." We cannot even say, "Our fathers got their water (faith) here in this manner." For the father of all faith-worship is Abraham who erected a shrine—to leave it behind. As the exegesis says, this does not mean the abstractions of a purely "spiritual" worship. It means that the past is important, we must make our *anamnesis*; it means that bread, wine, water, words, acts, are essential vehicles; it means that words can be more than just words, that a pew and an altar can be the gates of heaven, but precisely because they are *only* way-stations, and God is on the move, toward us, drawing us ever forward into a new realm.

The Third Sunday in Lent

Lutheran	*Roman Catholic*	*Episcopal*	*Pres./UCC/Chr.*	*Methodist/COCU*
Isa. 42:14-21	Ex. 17:3-7	Deut. 5:1, 6-21	Ex. 24:12-18	Ex. 17:3-7
Eph. 5:8-14	Rom. 5:1-2, 5-8	Rom. 8:1-10	Rom. 5:1-5	Rom. 8:1-10
John 9:1-41 (long)	John 4:5-42	John 9:1-13, 24-28	John 4:5-15	John 4:27-42
John 9:13-17, 34-39 (short)				

EXEGESIS

First Lesson: Isa. 42:14–21 (–23). The prophet whose words from the last years of the Babylonian Exile are collected in Isaiah 40–55 shares the deuteronomistic view of history that the disaster that had befallen Israel was the unavoidable consequence of its sin and disobedience. But he announces that Israel, "the Lord's Servant," will ultimately be exonerated (cf. the "servant songs" of this prophetical book). Deutero-Isaiah proclaims Israel's salvation in a mythological language which describes the coming events in cosmic dimensions, encompassing all of nature and all nations.

Isa. 42:14–17 is a self-contained unit which announces God's action in the near future. Isa. 42:18–21 belongs to a new unit which ends in 43:1–7 with an oracle of salvation. Its first part, 42:18–25, is among the most difficult sections of this prophetical book: the text is uncertain in many instances, there seem to be several glosses (42:19b, 21b, 24), and it is not possible to be certain about its character. Since questions which begin with "Who is . . . ?" (42:19) are typical of debates about the prophet's message (cf. 40:12, 13, 14), one could perhaps classify 42:18–25 as a discussion.

The second clause of 42:14 should be translated "shall I keep still and restrain myself forever?" The terms used here otherwise appear in public laments, sometimes also in hymns (cf. Ps. 28:1; 83:2; 85:6). In the second part of 42:14 the language changes: the picture of the woman in travail, here used of God himself, emphasizes the urgency and immediacy of God's action. Isa. 42:15 describes the general destruction that is caused by the fiery breath of the Lord in his coming; the countryside is turned into a desolate wilderness. Isa. 42:16 (the words "that they know not" and "that they have not known" are deleted by many commentators) continues this image, because it is the wilderness through which the people will be led "in a way" and "on a path." The wilderness is the place of darkness (cf. Jer. 2:6). The terms "blind" (and "see"), "darkness" and "light" signify in mythical language the radical reversal which the final hours of salvation will bring. The last clause of 42:16 underlines the certainty of God's determination. Isa. 42:17 is a later interpolation by someone who saw the destruction of the idol worshipers as an important part of the eschatological event.

Isa. 42:18–25 begins with a traditional prophetical appeal to the blindness and deafness of the people who refuse to listen to the message of God (cf. Isa. 6:9 f; Jer. 5:21; Ezek. 12:2)—not to be confused with the meaning of "blind" in 42:16. It is striking that the people accused as "blind" and "deaf" are nevertheless given the dignified title "servant of the Lord" (42:19). Not the Lord and King is blind—as some may have accused him, since he did not do anything for his people in exile—but the people themselves. Here, as in many passages of Deutero-Isaiah, "the Lord's servant" is not an individual, but the whole nation of Israel as the appointed representative of God on earth. In 42:19a, instead of "my messenger whom I sent," one should read "he who rules," i.e., God's servant who is destined to rule over the nations. Isa. 42:19b is repetitive, perhaps a later gloss. Isa. 42:20 quotes a proverb that ridicules people who never learn from their experiences. Such is Israel, and with such a servant God has to execute his rule on earth! Isa. 42:21, as it stands, does not make sense in this context. Deutero-Isaiah never speaks about the law in such terms; therefore "to magnify his law and make it glorious" should be deleted as a gloss and v. 21a connected with v. 22: "The Lord was pleased [to do it] for his righteousness sake, and now [his servant] is a people robbed and plundered. . . ." The rest of v. 22 contains a description of the disaster that God has brought upon his servant. Isa. 42:23 repeats the appeal of 42:18: After all that—who wants to listen? Since 42:24–25 contain fragments of a different character (or perhaps the people now speak, recognizing their situation), 43:1 connects directly with 42:23 as the proclamation of God's act of salvation which will restore the servant of the Lord to his dignity and honor. (So it is best to extend the reading to verse 23.)

Second Lesson: Eph. 5:8–14. The parenetical section of this epistle begins in 4:25 and ends in 6:9. It has two clearly distinguishable parts: (1) prohibitions (4:25–5:14); (2) instructions (5:15–6:9). The larger portion of the first part consists of an expanded catalogue of vices, not uncommon in Hellenistic Judaism and in early Christian writings (cf. Rom. 1:26–31; Gal. 5:19–21; Col. 3:5–6; etc.). The list of catalogue-prohibitions is interrupted in 4:32–5:2 where a positive admonition points to love as the basis of all Christian conduct: "walk in love as Christ loved us and gave himself up for us." Furthermore, a general admonition is added at the end of this first part of the parenesis, i.e., the verses which constitute the Second Lesson for this Sunday, Eph. 5:8–14.

The constitutive metaphors for the section 5:8–14 are "light" and "darkness." Such terminology is familiar in the Pauline Epistles, cf. Rom. 13:12; 2 Cor. 4:4–6; 1 Thess. 5:5. It is not merely figurative language: "light" is not a figurative word for moral values, nor is "darkness" for immorality. Rather "light" and "darkness" are metaphors which are drawn from the terminology of cosmological and religious dualism of the Hellenistic and Roman age. They designate realms diametrically opposed to each other. This can be expressed in terms of cosmic space: the heavenly world of light, and the lower world of darkness; or in terms of spirits: the spirit (or angel) of light and the spirit of darkness; or in terms of the battle between God and Satan. An example of such thinking is found in the Manual of Discipline of the Jewish sect from the Dead Sea: "The origin of truth is in a fountain of light, and the origin of perversity is from a fountain of darkness. Dominion over all the sons of righteousness is in the hand of the Prince of light. All dominion over the sons of perversity is in the hand of the Angel of darkness; they walk in the ways of darkness, . . ." (1 QS 3:19–24). To belong to either the realm of light or the realm of darkness is a fundamental fact which precedes all individual actions.

The Epistle to the Ephesians has combined this terminology with the Christian language of conversion "once—now" (5:8). Thus, partnership in the realm of light is not seen as a predetermined fate, nor as a share determined by nature. Conversion implies a transfer from one realm to the other. But it is the conduct of the Christians which establishes the reality of the realm of light and which separates light and darkness, whenever that which is good and right and true is done (5:9). "To take part" in the works of darkness—one could even translate "to become an accomplice"—would undo the transfer into the realm of light (5:11a). "To expose" (5:11b) is a legal term which means "to give conclusive evidence against something." In this way the battle between light and darkness takes place through the things which the Christians do (5:12–13).

The text concludes with the quotation of a hymnic fragment (5:14). It is probable that Clement of Alexandria has preserved the continuation of this hymn: "(Christ, the Lord) who is the sun of the resurrection, who was before the morning star, who grants life through his own rays" (*Protrepticus* 9.84.2). This hymn is a call to wake up. "To sleep" and "to wake up" are metaphors for life and death. Such calls in Christian texts are often associated with baptism (cf. Rom. 6:4). It is, therefore, possible that the whole text must be understood as an admonition to newly baptized Christians. In this context, the meaning of the last line of the hymn is not "that Christ will give light" to a new moral conduct, but that Christ "will arise as shining light" to the newly baptized (this is the more accurate translation of the rare Greek word which occurs here). Thus, the hymn serves as reminder that Christ has appeared to the Christians (cf. 2 Cor. 4:6), and they are now challenged to make this light visible in the world.

Gospel: John 9:1–41 (or 13–17, 34–39). This is one of the most carefully composed parts of this Gospel. Its basis is a traditional miracle story (the closest parallels occur in Mark 8:22–24 and 10:46–52). All the typical features of such stories are present. The encounter (9:1); the motivation for the healing as a response to a disciple's question raising the problem of sin and sickness—Jesus' answer is a typical motivation for such stories in John's Gospel, cf. 11:4, also 2:11: "they are manifestations of God's power" (9:2–3); the procedure of the healing: the use of spittle for an ointment is quite common in antiquity (cf. Mark 7:33; 8:23), also the command to wash, cf. 2 Kings 5:10 (John 9:6–7); and finally, the demonstration (9:8–9) and a return to Jesus, the healer (9:35–38; cf. Luke 17:11–19). It is this miracle story which the Gospel of John has used in order to create a number of scenes in which the beliefs and experiences of the church are reflected in the experiences of the man who was blind so that the work and ministry of Jesus become contemporaneous with the life of the believers.

(1) The first scene, 9:1–7, is highlighted by two statements of Jesus (9:4–5). Their text and meaning are not clear. One should probably read "*We* must work the works of him who sent *us*" (this reading is supported by Codex Sinaticus and by the recently discovered Papyrus 66). Thus the church is speaking here about the necessity to do the work of Jesus. "Day" and "night" are certainly not metaphors for "life" and "death," but for the time of "revelation" and the time of "condemnation" (cf. the use of the same metaphors in Rom. 13:11 f; 1 Thess. 5:1–10; see also John 11:9–10). What matters is to recognize the opportunity for salvation and to allow it to do its work, since salvation is "light," i.e., an active force in the world. There will be a time when this becomes impossible; not, of course, the time after Jesus' death, but the time when it is necessary to pronounce judgment and condemnation (cf. John 9:41!). There is one specific opportunity, the "day" for salvation to work—and not even serious religious considerations (as the one raised in 9:2) should be allowed to interfere. The following scenes exemplify both: the way of the blind man cured by Jesus and the way of the Pharisees who have been confronted with the work of the revelation (they "see"), but end in judgment.

The next four scenes are interrogations. The degree of hostility increases from one scene to the next; but the depth of the recognition of Jesus also progresses from scene to scene. (2) 9:8–12: The encounter of the cured man with the people. The cured man learns who Jesus is through their unbelief. In this scene he is only "the man called Jesus"; here there is no more than some doubt about Jesus' identity. (3) 9:13–17: The Pharisees appear as an official tribunal interrogating the cured man. Their questions seem to be objective and neutral. But it is not simply their aim to ridicule the possibility that Jesus could have done such a thing. They begin to build a wall of religious arguments against Jesus. If the blind are made to see, the age of the Messiah should be here. The criteria of established religion ("sinner" and Sabbath-breaker) prevent them from accepting the facts. But the man who was blind begins to see what is at stake and confesses: "He is a prophet." (4) 9:18–23: This second inquiry is not without humor. The attempt to establish that this man was not blind in the first place fails. This scene most clearly reflects the experiences of the church. A decision of the Jewish authorities to excommunicate all those who confess Jesus as Christ (cf. also John 12:42; 16:2) is presupposed, perhaps also the experience with friends who are unwilling to testify at a trial in behalf of the Christians. (5) 9:24–34: The third inquiry brings the controversy to a climax. Threats and methods of cross-examination are used. In the face of the ironic statement, "Do you too want to become his disciples?" the objectivity of the court breaks down. In 9:29 the Pharisees try to formulate a religious confession ("We know" is confessional style) in order to justify their opposition on religious grounds. In the answer of the cured man "we know" (9:31) occurs again: it is now the plural of the confessing church that speaks in the name of the true disciples of Moses. The statement ends in the acknowledgement that Jesus is from God (9:33). The subsequent outbreak of open hatred still tries to maintain the appearance of a serious religious position: "You are a sinner, since being born blind you are born in sin!" Of course, the statement is utterly ridiculous, since they themselves had doubted that he was born blind (9:18). At the same time, they now admit openly the truth of the healing event.

The last two scenes make Jesus the central figure. (6) 9:35–38: He is the Lord who is worshiped. For the title Son of man cf. John 1:51. It is evident that the preceding scenes said nothing about the psychology of the man who was blind; they spoke about the power and glory of Jesus as they were manifested in the experiences of believers. (7) 9:39–41 emphasizes the believers' task in the last scene in which Jesus confronts the Pharisees. The Pharisees have recognized the revelation and its claims and have rejected it. The play on the words "to see" and "to be blind" in these last verses makes the story of the blind man a symbol of the work of the church which is always the execution of the mission of Jesus. As those who have received sight, through the miracle that Jesus has accomplished, believers clarify their own faith in the encounter with the hostile world. In doing so, they expose for judgment (9:39) all those who reject, on the basis of their own religious convictions, the truth of Jesus' work that is there before their very eyes which are yet "blind" eyes.

HOMILETICAL INTERPRETATION

Introduction. There are two realms—one of darkness where nothing can be seen; one of light where all is clear and the way open. But two things must be noted. We can close our eyes, even in the light, and be in the dark as if there were no light. The dark is not a final, determined (cosmological) dark as in dualism but, as we shall see, under the dominion of the light. It is not a condominium of light and dark.

We know who has the dominion, but it is tragic beyond all words when the people of God themselves—Abraham's heirs, the very church —seems willfully to go with eyes closed, creating a land of darkness or of very fitful light. This is the theme of our three lessons: the light itself may be turned into darkness, but there is a way of life which belongs to the light, which is possible because the light cannot be engulfed (John 1:5). Moreover, we can know the Lord of the Light no matter what attempts are made by others to confuse us or to deny its reality. This is our message.

First Lesson. In Isaiah it is important to observe that the "servant" is primarily the people of God. That things have seemed to be going along undisturbed ("We're okay") is only because of the Lord God's restraint. But the longer the delusion lasts the more violent the eventual reaction. With the urgency and agony of the onset of childbirth the time arrives when things can no longer be contained; there will be a breaking-out (vv. 14–16). Then it will be seen that we have been living in a featureless wilderness, as lacking in markers as complete darkness. But the coming of the Lord which shatters and uproots all the accepted features of the landscape also turns it into a new country through which he will lead them into light.

One feature of darkness, as anyone knows who has groped about even a familiar house in the dark, is that nothing seems in the right place, small obstacles easily stepped over or around during the day "loom large" and provide major hazards. The light brings it all into proper relation, things in their places relative to each other, with proper space between, things in their proportionate dimension, easily avoided, readily found when needed. No matter how familiar, the dark makes it another realm and only the light can correct it. The light is another country and what lies far ahead is of more concern in the light than the right-at-hand (or at foot) with which we collide in the dark. In the dark even inanimate things seem demonic, as we have experienced in a sudden power-failure when there is no transforming light to switch on with the flip of a finger. Everything seems to conspire against us. There could hardly be a more apt "myth," a more appropriate symbol of our state and what is possible for us.

But Isaiah contains the warning (which becomes fully expressed in John 9:39) that some people choose darkness or half-light and wish others to live in that land, aliens from the realm of light. For self-created dark (or silence), where the light is actually shining (or the voice resounding), is serious, since what can be seen and has been seen (or heard) is rejected, pushed away into forgetfulness as though it did not exist (v. 20). This is the plight of a people who were meant themselves to be the leaders of others into the light, reflecting the light into the dark by showing that they are where one can find the way ahead, that they live in a land where things are in proper perspective and place.

Whatever the confusion of v. 21 (see exegesis), our reading ends here. Unless extended to v. 23, it may best be treated as an assertion of God's self-directed will, not dependent on any particular "servant" (people or church), a will capable of finding another, capable even of "redeeming" the chosen one, though only a few, or only one, is found willing to have eyes opened, ears unstopped, to accept the light where the way appears and to live in that land and move that way. The one who does this does it for the benefit of all who come to a standstill, bewildered and needing the assurance of light.

Once again the preacher must seriously examine himself as to how fully he lives in the light, with eyes gladly open, and must speak as one who shares the experience of the need for light and affirms for his people that it is there to be found, even though none of us have fully claimed our heritage. That is the theme of the Second Lesson.

Second Lesson. Here we are in a different age, a new world. The light has come and cannot be dispelled—though it seemingly can still be abandoned. Notice we are back to the "now," the nowness which replaces the "once" (see Ash Wednesday). The gospel, as a former colleague used to urge, is not hortatory but declaratory, not the imperative but the indicative, not "ought" but "is." In truly Pauline fashion the author has declared the faith-basis, reaching back into God's eternal purpose, as the ground for a new mode of life and unity. Like Paul, here he liberally uses the "Therefore" (4:1, 25; 5:1 and even 7). The "parenesis," or exhortation, is grounded in and through Christ and that absolute faith in Christ stands, and in that faith is where *we* stand. As the exegesis suggests, baptism may well have been a recent experience for these hearers or readers. It was all new. We should probably think of them as pagans, Gentiles, as well as Jews who had undergone instruction (a catechumenate) and made a decision to accept Christian baptism as the once and for all mark of a radical break with a totally different way of life. How hard for us, where the shadow of Christendom still lingers, to recapture the impact of such a transition, such a migration.

For that is what it was—a stepping ashore into the land of light from the dark and threatening waters of the past. It is not simply a move into a lighted area, but the dark itself has become the light itself and so only a term such as "rebirth" will serve. (Which is, after all, what the baptismal act sets forward as a sign.) Just as what makes visible is the light, so also what is made visible is light. It serves as light because it is lighted. All that is "good and right and true" is the "fruit" of light as Christians are "children" of, that is, generated by the light. It is as though we had been asleep, even dead, and have been awakened or raised up to find ourselves in a realm of light, the source and radiance of which is Christ.

What that first generative result is, how it is seen, is spelled out in Ephesians. As the light brings things into proportion and relation with each other, so the move into the land of light involves a new "seeing" of all relationships. All is illuminated within and without. We become willing to "open ourselves" and are able now to move with a sure tread. We can *see*, or have begun to. (The preacher can readily think of actual cases from his reading or observation of Christian lives.)

Yet the dark is still there; it has its own ways. Having been dark ourselves, we find that the habitual ways of the dark are hard to break away from. But the light shows them up for the darkness they are; it exposes the darkness of the dark.

Anyone who chooses the light stands exposed. This has its dangers but it is also opportunity. Light has the most power to attract of anything there is. Our "lighted" way of life, our "illumined" acts are witness. We are children of the light, yes, but also its servants. How miraculous a light seems on a dark deserted road. It speaks safety, comfort, humanity —above all, company. How, in a power-failure, we cluster about those who have independent sources of light. How we are greeted as saviors, almost, if we can produce a glow in a darkened house, find the switch that ties us into the source and illuminates even this abode when the connection is made.

Note the use of the word "accomplice" in the exegesis of Eph. 5:11a. To accept, to continue, to imitate the works of the dark is to be dark. Yet the Christian knows what the dualists seem not to have known, that the dark has no final reality. For our world the dark is the shadow of the earth itself, cast onto itself, caused by the light of the sun. The turning will bring us again into the light and that is the final, the all-determining reality. The rest is but the shadow of its rejection.

Lent can be for the already baptized a time of reaffirmation of baptismal light as well as, for others, a catechumenate. (It might be well to discuss the Second Lesson and the Gospel in reverse order.)

Gospel. The blind man, released into a world of light and people (whom he can now see), is the Christian and the church itself, taking a stand against efforts to reject and confuse, against attempts to discredit the source of the new light. There are many strands, many levels to this story, so that it is unwise to use all of them in one sermon. The abbreviated passage may be necessary for reading, but in preaching the whole story should be in mind and communicated, if only step by step, in a series of sermons.

When the man can for the first time "see" there are those who want to tell him what (and whom) he sees. They are especially concerned about the way he may see Jesus. The man comes to that by stages, a gradual clearing of his own understanding, forced on him in part by the attempts of others to make him question his own perception of the situation. We may for brevity refer to "the man" but bear in mind (see exegesis) that he represents the Christian experience and fellowship, just as the opponents represent the synagogue. Though this story deals with the conflict between them over the question of Jesus and is not a psychological study, we can hardly think or speak of it without using modern terms.

In our language "identity" is involved. The man has no "identity crisis" but the religious leaders try to impose one on him (vv. 8–9, 18–21). As a result the man comes to a fuller grasp of his own new identity which he recognizes depends on Jesus, to whom he must ultimately return. Finally, it is his understanding of who "the healer" is, the true identity of Jesus, which is at stake, as his opponents well understand. They are forced to abandon their efforts to disprove the facts (vv. 15, 18, 24, 26 ff.) and so resort to discrediting the originator of the new situation (as in Mark 3:22 and parallels; a technique not unknown to our own Senate investigating committees). The "establishment" could not impose an identity crisis on the man, nor get his stalwart parents to help, because Jesus had given the man the knowledge of what his new identity was—a blind man delivered from blindness, now able to see (v. 25). By the mercy of God he would retain this sense of the basic fact of deliverance.

They tried to create an identity crisis about Jesus for anyone tempted to recognize and so follow him. "We do not know who he is . . . where he is from." The fallacy of origins in a new form (John 1:45, 46; 7:50–52), religious snobbery at a new depth. The Gospels suggest that it was thought that the Messiah, when he came, would bear some marks of his divine origin, some device establishing his identity rather than "by his works you will know him." We must not underestimate the reality of the problem for the Jewish church faced with Christians. Jesus is to be discredited because he does not observe the religious ground rules—and presumably neither does the church. It is not a dead problem. The radical "Christianizing" of the churches is opposed by those outside as well as by some within on the grounds of inherited but peripheral judgments —moralistic, formal, ritualistic. We have our own "Sabbath hang-ups."

How well we see depends on what we see or, being human, primarily on whom we see (how we evaluate those within our range). Who most nearly fills our vision? To whom do we turn to understand others? By being Christians we come to know that to be truly persons, truly mature, our vision must be filled with Christ. As he is our Light so, in a sense, he becomes our eyes. The man's parents were content to let the man's vision take in what he had to from his new seeing-point—unlike some who wish children's eyes to be full of themselves. The child's vision, like that of the man who newly sees, must range freely and further to be fully mature. The man, now on his own, liberated from dependence, seeking liberation from those who would dictate his religious experience, now moves, or is forced, from stage to stage. "The man called Jesus did it" (v. 11)—"I do not know where he is" (v. 12)—"this is what he did" (v. 15)—"even if he breaks rules, he is a prophet" (v. 17)—"I do not know whether he is a 'sinner,' but I know he changed me from blind to seeing" (v. 25)—"do you want to become his disciples?" (v. 27—is he admitting this is the only alternative for him himself?)—"why bother about questions like 'where he comes from' when he can open eyes?" (v. 30)—"it is impossible that he is not 'from God'" (v. 33). Then the man is classified a sinner along with Jesus (Christians must bear the stigma of association with outcasts even as his apostles were found "guilty by association" in Acts 4:13). Do opponents sometimes more readily than Christians themselves recognize that the essence of being a Christian is identity with Christ?

So there is a "return to Jesus." Jesus seeks out the man and asks of him a "confession" (see exegesis). The man can only express his willingness and in response Jesus discloses himself no longer as simply the one who does but as the one who is. The man now confesses his faith and it turns to worship. (Note here how the stages of the rite of baptism are essentially followed.) This is the experience of the church and of Christians. There is always a return to Jesus, though we drift away, are deflected, are excluded from the confidence of others, there is always the power of Christ to attract, to re-attract, to attract again, until we recognize his claim on us, his seeking us out, and admit that he is the source of our light. The identity crisis of the Christian is, only and ultimately, resolved by Christ becoming our identity.

The Fourth Sunday in Lent

Lutheran	Roman Catholic	Episcopal	Pres./UCC/Chr.	Methodist/COCU
Hos. 5:15-6:2	1 Sam. 16:1b, 6-7, 10-13a	Deut. 8:7-18	2 Sam. 5:1-5	1 Sam. 16:1b, 6-7, 10-13a
Rom. 8:1-10	Eph. 5:8-14	Rom. 8:11-19	Eph. 5:8-14	Eph. 5:8-14
Matt. 20:17-28	John 9:1-41	John 6:4-15	John 9:1-11	John 9:1-41

EXEGESIS

First Lesson: Hos. 5:15–6:2. The first verse of this lesson concludes a series of threats and accusations against Ephraim (5:8–15). The remainder belongs to a psalm of repentance, 6:1–3. Another long series of accusations responds to the song of repentance (6:4–7:16). The whole section 5:8–7:16 reflects a very specific historical situation, most probably the year 733/2 B.C. in the Northern kingdom of Israel (=Ephraim), i.e., ten years before the final destruction of that kingdom through the Assyrians. In the preceding years the king of Israel, Pekah, had made an alliance with Rezin, the king of Damascus, against the Assyrians. When the king of Judah refused to join this alliance, Pekah and Rezin invaded Judah, but could not conquer Jerusalem. Tiglath-Pileser III of Assyria would not allow such dangerous developments, led his army into Syria-Palestine, conquered Damascus, invaded the northern districts of the kingdom of Israel (Galilee) and threatened to destroy Samaria. At this point, a certain Hoshea, son of Elah, murdered King Pekah of Israel, usurped the kingship for himself and resumed the paying of tribute to the Assyrians; cf. 2 Kings 15:30.

The prophet Hosea refers to these events (cf. 7:3, 7, 13), and also mentions that Israel had tried to get help from Egypt (Hos. 7:11). The achievements of the king who had secured some sort of peace find no acknowledgment in Hosea's prophecies. On the contrary, he proclaims that the prospects for the future are very bad indeed. From the south the king of Judah will invade the country (Hos. 5:8 f; 7:16). But Judah also is threatened by the Lord's wrath (5:12–14). The same God who once had promised salvation and protection to his people has become their terrible enemy. In daring and bold metaphors God is described as a wild and terrible lion who destroys his people (5:14). The section concludes with a new image which is probably drawn from oriental myth: The Lord withdraws and goes away, while the final destruction of his people is taking place (5:15). "Until they acknowledge their guilt" (RSV) is a mistranslation; one must translate "until they have been punished."

Hos. 6:1–3 is the quotation of a song of repentance as it may have been sung on a day of public confession at Samaria (cf. 1 Sam. 7:5–6). Songs of public repentance are preserved in Pss. 79; 85:5–8; 90:13–17. Like the last two of these examples, Hos. 6:1–3 also lacks the elements of confession of sin and admission of guilt, and there are no vows and promises. Instead we find statements of trust and confidence. Thus, this song represents popular piety which speaks of God in images of striking contrast to those used by the prophet in 5:14. Hos. 6:1 seems to comply with the prophetic request "to return," but cf. Hos. 5:4! In 6:2 one should translate "he will keep us alive" (not "he will revive us"). "After two days, . . . on the third day" designates a very short period of time. Though there were myths of oriental fertility deities which told that the deities would rise after two days, or on the third day, it is unlikely that these phrases intend to allude to them. "He will raise us up" does not speak about raising from the dead, but about raising up from the sick bed. Hos. 6:3 is a very clear expression of beliefs which understood the actions of the Lord of Israel's history in analogy to fertility deities.

Hos. 6:4 begins the response of the prophet to such entirely inadequate repentance. Insofar as this verse is formulated in the style of the priestly oracle (cf. Ps. 85:9), it still reflects the proper liturgical response. However, God, speaking through the prophet, refuses to grant forgiveness. The use of nature imagery ridicules such repentance and its naive assumptions. God is the Lord of History who is slaying and judging his people (6:5); he cannot be appeased like a fertility deity. "Love instead of sacrifice" (6:6) formulates clearly the basic theological position of the prophetical critique of the bankrupt political establishment. Unless Israel is able to make this position its own, there will not be any salvation.

Second Lesson: Rom. 8:1–10 (11). In the preceding chapter of the epistle Paul had spoken of the freedom from the law. Chap. 8 treats the freedom from sin and death through the power of the Spirit. Rom. 8:1–39 is a unit that shows a clear disposition: (1) Life in the Spirit as freedom from the flesh, 8:1–11; (2) Life in the Spirit as sonship, 8:12–17; (3) the Spirit in the eschatological situation, 8:19–30; (4) the love of Christ as eschatological victory, 8:31–39. The lesson for this Sunday should be extended to include 8:11.

For the understanding of this text, the terms "flesh" and "spirit" are decisive. "Spirit," in the ancient world, is divine power; it is connected with miracle and ecstasy; it is a power that breaks into this established world as it destroys, moves, builds up, and inspires so that people experience a reality which they can neither produce nor master by their own means. The realm of human control, on the other hand, is called "flesh," and it includes everything that is tangible and visible. Through the dualistic view of the world at that time "spirit" and "flesh" were seen as diametrically opposed to each other. "Flesh" became the realm of everything temporary, weak, passing, and destructible; "spirit" designated that which was strong, everlasting, eternal. Anthropologically "spirit" was understood as the true divine self of human beings, "flesh" as the mortal physical body. Paul depends on this terminology, but human beings with all they have and with all they are, body, soul, and mind, are subject to the power of "flesh," caught in a vicious circle in which the law prods them to do what earns life, only in order to demonstrate to them that they are working death for themselves even if they fulfill the law (Rom. 7:7–25). "Spirit" appears in opposition to this realm of human possibilities, including the law. Paul refuses to connect the "Spirit" either to the human mind or to the realm of morality and order that is represented by the law. But if the "Spirit" is God's eschatological gift to the church, given to every Christian in baptism (1 Cor. 12:13), what are its manifestations?

Rom. 8:1 states that being "in Christ Jesus," i.e., in the church, puts an end to all condemnation (eschatological judgment). Some translations add: "who walk not after the flesh, but after the Spirit"—a secondary expansion which only occurs in some manuscripts. The thematic statement for the whole passage is given in 8:2. "Law of the Spirit" is the determining *power* of the eschatological situation, not a new moral or ritual law. Therefore, the realization of this Spirit in the life of the Christians is not called obedience, but freedom, i.e., freedom from the realm of sin and death with which the "law" is closely associated. Rom. 8:3 should be translated: "What was impossible for the law, where it was powerless [weak] because of the flesh—God has sent his son . . ." Paul does not complete the first sentence, but breaks if off abruptly in order to juxtapose a statement which is an expanded credal formula (cf. Gal. 4:4; John 3:16 f). The positive counterpart to the law is, thus, not the power of the Spirit, but rather what God has done through Christ, i.e., an event of cosmic dimensions of victory and judgment that took place on the cross. This fulfilled the "just requirement of the law" (8:4) in such a way that "we who walk not according to the flesh, but according to the Spirit" became part of this event through our own conduct.

Old and new conduct are both described as "to set one's mind on something," either the flesh or the Spirit. The term "law," however, only occurs when Paul speaks about the old conduct (8:7). Similarly, the words "submit" and "can" (cf. the double "cannot" in 8:7 and 8) occur only here. But for those who are "in the spirit" (8:9a) it is no longer a question of the "ability" to please or of "submission" to the law, but rather a question of new being (8:9b). It is a life after death in which all Christians participate. This is expressed in 8:10–11 through a formulation which alludes to baptism (cf. Rom. 6:1–10). As the Christians have thus physically experienced death to sin (analogous to Christ's crucifixion, cf. above 8:3), they are now in a life in which righteousness (of God!) is a reality (8:10). As in Romans 6, the resurrection from the dead is still an event expected in the future; but the Spirit of the God who raised Jesus is already a power in those mortal bodies which will at once be made alive (8:11).

Gospel: Matt. 20:17–28. This pericope consists of two different sections: (1) "The Third Prediction of the Passion", Matt. 20:17–19, (2) "Christ and the Sons of Zebedee," Matt. 20:20–28. In both parts, Matthew follows his source, the Gospel of Mark (cf. Mark 10:32–34 and 10:35–45). Mark highlighted the central section of his Gospel by three predictions of the passion of Jesus: Mark 8:31–33; 9:30–32; 10:32–34. All three reflect the structure of early Christian credal formulas about Jesus being handed over, crucified, and raised after three days. Mark sees the "confessing church" as Jesus' company on the way to Jerusalem, especially emphasized in this last prediction of the passion where Mark speaks of the amazement and fear of those who accompany Jesus.

The second section, Matt. 20:20–28 (=Mark 10:35–45) is a more complex composition. Originally, it must have been a simple paradigm which was used in the church for preaching and instruction, consisting of the question about honors in the future kingdom (Matt. 20:21) and of an answer in the form of a saying of Jesus which is probably preserved in Matt. 20:23b (=Mark 10:40). Its purpose was to point out that it was not Jesus' business to promise honors in the kingdom of God, but that it was God's own right. This original paradigm was expanded in three different ways. (1) Matt. 20:24–27 (from Mark 10:41–44)—directed to all disciples—says that greatness in the kingdom of God is not to be measured by secular criteria. On the contrary, greatness is service. Matthew emphasizes the rejection of secular criteria when he uses the terms "lord it over" and "exercise authority" which imply the abuse of power. Compare the version of this saying in the Gospel of Luke: here the "lords" and "benefactors"—frequent titles of emperors and other dignitaries in the Roman world—are contrasted with the "nobodies" of the church, i.e., young people and servants (Luke 22:25). (2) Another saying about service is added in Matt. 20:28 (from Mark 10:45). It is formulated to conform with the understanding of the title "Son of man" as it appears in the predictions of the passion. Luke 22:27 preserves an older version in which the title "Son of man" was not yet used. Jesus is not simply an example of "serving," but the one who accomplishes the work of the redeemer through his service, i.e., through his death. "Serving" is, therefore, no longer the opposite of "being master" and "being served by others," but is identical with giving oneself for the freedom of all people. The Greek word translated "ransom" occurs in the NT only here (and in the parallel Mark 10:45; a synonymous word appears in 1 Tim. 2:6). The meaning of this term is: "the price paid to buy freedom," as, e.g., in the freeing of slaves or prisoners. "Freedom" can mean freedom from sin (Hebr. 9:15) or deliverance from earthly life (Rom. 8:23), but normally it is freedom as such (cf. Luke 21:28; Eph. 4:30). Also Matt. 20:28 speaks in general of the paradox that "serving buys freedom"—but a service that consists of giving one's life; it gives what a master cannot control. (3) The last addition to the original paradigm appears in Matt. 20:22–23a (from Mark 10:38–39—but Matt. leaves out the sentences about the "baptism," cf. Luke 12:50). The "drinking of the cup" refers to death; it predicts a martyr's death for these disciples. The later church has given the martyrs special honors as "saints" who are elevated above the average Christians. In the context of this pericope, even martyrs appear without special rights.

As Matthew used these various traditions which had been composed into a unit by Mark, he made several significant changes of his own. In Matt. 20:17 he wrote: "he took the twelve disciples aside." Only for those who follow Jesus and who are bought into freedom by him does the mysterious relationship between Jesus' "service" and the disciples' fate make sense. This text addresses "inner-Christian" problems. In 20:20 (cf. 20:21) Matthew introduces the mother of the sons of Zebedee as the one who brings the request for the place of honor for her sons. Ambitions which arise out of secular social structures enter into the experience of the church. Thus, there is a greater awareness of the ways in which the unity is threatened that exists mysteriously between Jesus service and their own task of freedom by service to each other.

HOMILETICAL INTERPRETATION

Traditionally this was known as "Refreshment Sunday" (also Laetare and Mothering Sunday). In this cycle the relief appears in the form of a focus on expectation rather than on the ancient theme of the feeding in the wilderness, but the theme of freedom is maintained. Once again it will probably be wise to treat the Gospel Lesson before Paul's exposition.

The exegesis lays the ground for treating the short passage from Hosea as a typical expression of penitence about which the prophet proceeds to express his doubts. The "song" has nothing to do with the resurrection—unless recovery from wounding and sickness can be considered a resurrection. The terms have become so grounded in the Christianizing of the OT that it may be difficult to escape the words "revive" and "after two days . . . on the third." The latter is a common mode of expression suggesting something like "almost immediately" (see its use in Luke 13:32–33) in contrast to the longer "forty days" we encountered earlier.

It is easy in stress or dire straits to "return" to the Lord (still easier to call for such return), to express the hope of a restoration too quickly, and to look for an almost immediate end of the problems. The "naive assumption," "Maybe it will go away," seems to be the level on which the prophet hears the popular response. That response itself is like morning clouds, like dew, metaphors for what is soon dissipated. The dealings of God are not like that nor can the dealing with God be. (See the climax of the protest in 6:6.) Yet turning, revivification, and living before God are proper steps, ingredients, prospects in an act of faith if they are not a mere "song" but result from an encounter with the realities of our situation, not from our prospects but from God's infinitely higher intention for us. So the Hosea passage, without distortion into typological prophecy of the resurrection, may be treated as an introduction to the expectations theme in Matthew and Romans.

I would go further than Dr. Koester in believing that the imagery of the journey to Jerusalem (the way of the Christian disciple) and the warnings of Christ (the martyrdom theme) go back to a genuine recollection in Mark of false expectations on the part of Jesus' friends about what lay ahead in Jersualem and about Jesus' intention in going there. However that may be, the expectations of the followers of Jesus—even in the Lenten pilgrimage—may be misdirected. "Jerusalem the golden," yes, but that is transformation. Jerusalem with thrones for the faithful (the Twelve—see Matt. 19:28) belongs to eschatology (the "palingenesis"). Not thrones, but a cross which denies to the victim the pretense even of humanness in its cruel distortion and helplessness. The paradox of Christian faith is the cross become the (earthly) throne of Christ the (heavenly) King. But the cross is there, to be negotiated, accepted, turned from fact into paradox. And the servant can expect nothing different from his lord—not literal crucifixion, but to "be baptized" and "to drink the cup" meant at least readiness to go the final step if called on to do so, to shirk no experience no matter how bitter, to expect, in a sense, the worst before the reviving, the healing, the raising up to newness of life could come.

If this Sunday the stress is on what is to be endured before revival comes, next Sunday will remind us that the cross has to be seen in the light of resurrection, not alone. But that change of perspective, necessary before the plunge into Passiontide, assumes that the cross and the way to it are still real, and must have a place in the expectations of the Christian. The expectant aspect is that the cross is itself, as our Roman brethren would say, "salvific"—since it is the cross of Jesus Christ. This would bring us directly to Paul; but first look again at Matthew.

A word of caution is in order: by ignoring redaction as clear as Matthew's a preacher can undermine his reliability in the eyes of well educated listeners. If any stress is to be put on the request of the mother (as Matthew has it, in contrast to Mark where the request is made directly by James and John) it should be made clear that the preacher is aware it is a deliberate change on Matthew's part, whether in the interest of "saving-face" for two, by now, apostolic figures, or as a suggestion that family or social pressure can influence expectations, the expressions of aims.

Just what the expectation of Jesus, historically, was in confronting Jerusalem and the establishment there may be lost in obscurity. But Jesus' view now appears for us only in the Christianized versions of the "Passion Predictions." His reply to the request of the "Sons of Thunder" may be transposed into the key of Christian martyrdom, but at least it is a reminder that death itself (even that "failure") may be within God's purpose, may be "redeemable," subject to "ransom" (see exegesis of the Second Lesson). We may well be staggered (and why not?) at this hint of the dimensions of Jesus' faith that God truly is sovereign and can turn the ultimate disaster into the means of salvation. After all, as Paul proposes, the issue is a deep and fundamentally tragic one ("condemnation") that is to be dealt with by no ordinary means if God's purpose ("no condemnation") is to be achieved. (But let us not, please, get into grim theories of atonement, Anselmic or other).

The expectations imposed on us by life and culture ("way of life," American or otherwise; "life-style," malformed ideas of "freedom") are the legitimate objects of scrutiny under the Christian proclamation. They are deeply ingrained (even in the preacher!) and cannot be simply "sprinkled with holy water." We easily get back to "Father Adam" rather than "Father Abraham" (previous Sundays) because the expectations we are culturally expected to share contain a large ingredient of self-help, no matter what the religious label affixed advertises. It is the final expectation and how it is to be arrived at that characterizes the difference of Christian faith-life—its "style", its expectations all along the way.

Salvation is freedom; that is clearly Paul's insistence. But freedom from what? Here, in this connection, from false expectations: that grace is cheap, that there will be rewards for heroic effort (we reward ourselves or is it God's grace?); that what we already know will determine, and so limit, what may be expected. Paul talks about this in one word, aptly translated "to set your mind on." That is it. What is the "mind-set" of the Christian to be? Not easy to answer. Not because we are uneducated, insufficiently cathechized, have not done our homework, have not sufficiently analyzed the problem to see the solution (incorrectly programmed the computer). Not for any such reasons is the answer impossible of reduction to an equation, a formula, much less a slogan. Instead, because, to use an unusable word, it is "eschatological." It is, could we say again "open-ended." It allows, in expecting, for the unexpected, indeed, for the unpredictable. "Eye has not seen, nor ear heard." Or in the terms of an ancient collect, "O God, who has prepared for those who love thee such good things *as pass man's understanding* . . . . that we . . . . may obtain thy promises which exceed all that *we can desire.*"

Success, problem-solving, grounds our expectation. Grounds it literally, holding it to the already known, the already formulated (even liturgically), the already anticipated, the earthly. But even science seems no longer able to live with exactly that. Literature and the arts have long been in protest. We have all, maybe, been "Waiting for Godot." There are many "indicators"—beside the revolts of youthful counter-culture—in the sheer facts of the environment, in the ennui, satiation, and disillusion creeping up with wide spreading affluence, that "success" is not satisfying to humans, that achievement has somewhere a hollow core, that we have not set ourselves free by assuring ourselves we do not condemn ourselves (and that God does not either—*c'est son metier*—it is God's thing!).

Paul's revelation was other than that. We have that "now" again.

"There is then, *now,* no condemnation . . . ." But there was. Not now, "for those in Christ Jesus." There, in Christ Jesus, is found the spirit of life, a new, "now," situation which has set us free. The time has come (in this Lent cycle) to lift up the whole matter into promise and hope and the exhilaration of freedom. If only Christians as such, could exhibit some exhilaration (near even to "hilarity"—in both Latin and Greek) of freedom. It cannot be achieved by rule ("law"), not by patching up what we have and are (that would be to be "patterned," but we are called to break the mold, not schematized but metamorphosized, Rom. 12:2).

The mind-set of the flesh, Paul says, has us gripped in a vise, the jaws of which are sin and death. But all this is (now) changed. Christ has come, God's "own Son" has come, fully, intimately acquainted with our condition, so that what all religion set out to accomplish might actually happen when we move (or are moved) into the realm of the Spirit.

Paul has lots to say about this for it embraces the whole Christian life and "personality." We know we are in this realm of Spirit when we are "in Christ." It is impossible to be there without having the Spirit of Christ. This again can so easily be reduced to a formality. But it is the "mind-set" that reveals the reality of it all. It manifests itself in many ways—the extremes of terminology will not exhaust it ("life" vs. "death," "hostility" vs. "peace," etc.), the varieties of personality make it inexpressible, as do the swiftly changing facts of circumstance. In today's reading we can find *one* way to sum it all up—the expectant life.

The Christian (in the Spirit, by the Spirit, the Spirit in him or her) has a new "openness" to experience. Expectation cannot be limited. Experience may be limited, but breaking out of common experience comes the unexpected (unplanned) new aspect, new relationship, new feel, new tone—how describe it? If you have known it you know what is meant. It can be seen in others. The Christian experiences new possibilities, fresh coincidences (others would call them that), a sort of newly revealed glow to the commonplace because he is expectant, "open to" the reality that God's Spirit is at work. This openness, expectancy, cannot be planned, but it can be nurtured by prayer, to which Paul moves on, showing how the Spirit speaks for us before we formulate the words. This is the characteristic of the mind-set of the Spirit. An open expectancy, freed from the dictates of the rigidly programmed and limited nature of the "flesh," open to the new end which cannot be defined. (Unless it be defined as Christ. Julian of Norwich understood this; she frequently spoke of being "right merry," when she wrote "I 'liked' no other heaven than Jesus".)

Our bodies are, as Paul insists, "mortal"—faced with the end of death—but the Spirit is already among us, the Spirit of the God who is known as the God who raised Jesus from the dead, and the end that is death is another opening of expectancy, the expectancy of more life yet. But it is only bodily dying we have to do and we can, in a sense, anticipate that, so that life is left, the Spirit given, the indwelling-life, as our fundamental expectation. In sorrow, in woe, in confusion, in decay, in limitations, with Spirit-expectancy life breaks through—now.

The Fifth Sunday in Lent

Lutheran	*Roman Catholic*	*Episcopal*	*Pres./UCC/Chr.*	*Methodist/COCU*
Ezek. 37:1-3 (4-10), 11-14	**Ezek. 37:12-14**	**Ezek. 37:1-3, 11-14**	**Ezek. 37:11-14**	**Ezek. 37:1-3, 11-14**
Rom. 8:11-19	**Rom. 8:8-11**	**Rom. 8:31b-39**	**Rom. 8:6-11**	**Rom. 8:6-11**
John 11:1-53 (long)	**John 11:1-45**	**John 11:18-44**	**John 11:1-4, 17, 34-44**	**John 11:1-45**
John 11:47-53 (short)				

EXEGESIS

First Lesson: Ezek. 37:1–3 (4–10) 11–14. This text comprises one of the great visions of the Book of Ezekiel (cf. Ezek. 1:1–3: 15; 8:1–11:25; 40–42). The time is the early period of the exile in Babylon (after 587 B.C.). The text has two parts: the vision, 37:1–10; the interpretation and message, 37:11–14. Both parts belong closely together. The connection is provided by 37:11 where a statement of despair is quoted: "Our bones are dried up . . ." This statement is the source of the vision, but also the cause for the prophetic message in 37:12–14.

As in other visions of Ezekiel, the prophet is not a passive observer, but he takes an active role; cf. 2:8–3:3 where he has to swallow a book (see also 8:7–9). Here he must speak the words of prophecy which accomplish the dramatic events of the vision. The bones in the valley are dried up by the sun; thus, the question, "Can these bones live?" is almost cynical as it emphasizes the terrible reality of death. The answer (37:3) does not imply any belief in the resurrection, but expresses both the human lack of power in the face of death and the belief in God's power to do the impossible. The prophet himself is requested to announce God's will. The words which he has to speak are in form and function prophetical calls. Thus this scene does not symbolize some divine miracle beyond time and history, but an act of God to be accomplished through his messenger. The reviving of the dead bones in two separate actions is reminiscent of the creation of man in Gen. 2:7. First the physical human being is restored (an interesting physiological knowledge is revealed here), then the breath of life is given (37:4–8 and 9–10). The life-giving breath is represented by the four winds, probably a mythological concept of Babylonian origin (the breath is not the Spirit of God or a divine soul).

The vision is explained to the prophet, it is not proclaimed to Israel (37:11). Its purpose was solely to reassure the prophet that God is powerful even in such a hopeless situation as the dead and dried-up bones of slain people depict. It is Israel in its cast-down state that he has seen, as Israel itself has described its situation with the words "Our bones are dried up"—figurative language for sorrow, suffering, and weakness (cf. Ps. 31:10; Prov. 17:22). The message uses a different imagery: "raise you from your graves." It continues with another traditional theme that speaks of the exodus and of the promised land (37:12–13). Ezek. 37:14, "I will put my spirit within you" recalls the prophecy of Ezek. 36:26–27 which resumes the proclamation of the famous Jer. 31:33 passage. The final clause, "I have spoken and I have done it" (Ezek. 37:14; cf. 36:36), underlines God's determination and excludes the possibility that normal political developments might bring a reversal of Israel's fate.

This text from Ezekiel does not know the later belief in an eschatological resurrection of the dead, although many Jewish and Christian interpreters have understood it as such a prophecy. It is rather a powerful and radical proclamation of God's will. Life will come to the people through the act of God, but never through the human exploitation of existing possibilities. Neither does such divine action presuppose favorable historical conditions, nor does it ask for moral or religious qualifications. Only from a new creation which parallels the original act of creation (Gen. 2:7) can Israel expect the life out of death. This new creation will not only repeat what God has done in the past, it will do much more. It will give a new spirit which is God's own Spirit.

Second Lesson: Rom. 8:11–19. It is advisable to limit this lesson to vv. 12–17. Rom. 8:11 is still part of the conclusion of the preceding pericope, 8:1–11; and the last verses begin a new section which treats of the Spirit in the eschatological situation (8:18–30). On this and on the meaning of the terms "spirit" and "flesh," see the exegesis of the Second Lesson for the Fourth Sunday in Lent above.

Rom. 8:12–17 characterizes life in the Spirit as sonship. Rom. 8:1–11 had identified the believers with the experience and the dimension of the death and life of Jesus through whom God had judged the powers of sin. Rom. 8:12–17 focuses on that term through which the new status of the believers is most appropriately described: sonship. "So then" in 8:12 intends to draw a positive conclusion from the statement in 8:10–11. But the term "debtors" is not adequate to describe the life in the Spirit (cf. Gal. 5:3). Thus, Paul only adds a negative characterization: "not to the flesh . . ." The phrase "according to the flesh" does not only refer to the "fleshly desires," but to the entire movement of life which is self-directed in the pursuit of innerworldly objectives. Death is a necessary consequence (8:13a; cf. 1 Cor. 7:31). Life is, therefore, only possible in the constant "putting to death" of the deeds of that self (="body," 8:13b). Paul is a realist. Human beings cannot escape into becoming pure spirits. But they are "driven by the Spirit" as if by a great force (8:14). The translation "led by the Spirit" is too weak, and no moralistic implications are intended by Paul.

Paul speaks of the assembled congregation that has received the Spirit through baptism. It is in this congregation that the liturgical acclamation "Abba! Father!" (8:16) gives witness that God's Spirit is present. "Abba" is an Aramaic liturgical call; one must compare it with the Aramaic liturgical calls "Amen" and "Maranatha" (1 Cor. 16:22). There is no reference to the Lord's prayer, nor has the address "Abba" any connotations of personal familiarity (it does not mean "Daddy"). This public manifestation of God's presence through the Spirit in the assembled congregation gives witness to (or "together with") our "Spirit," i.e., the Spirit given to each Christian in baptism (the word "Spirit" must be capitalized in both instances in 8:17a). As the synonymous words "sons" and "children" speak of an eschatological reality, so, too, "heirs"—originally referring to the promised land—is an eschatological term. Again the christological aspect is emphasized: "fellow-heirs with Christ," which is identical with the expected "glorification with him" (8:17b). As the following verses (8:18 ff) indicate, "the sufferings of the present times" are a part of the Christians' share in the futility and bondage of the whole creation. "Suffering" refers to the realities of life in this world in general—as the powers of the flesh and the deeds of the body remain a continuing threat to Christian life and conduct. Again in this case, it is the Spirit, God's power, which sustains the believers in hope—a hope for future victory over the adversities of life which already qualifies the experience of the present.

Gospel: John 11:1–53. The section from John 10:40 to 11:54 constitutes the conclusion of Jesus' public ministry. It is framed by two schematic remarks about Jesus' travel, 10:40–42 and 11:54; both present Jesus as going away to a remote place and thus underline the special significance of this story. Indeed, Jesus' coming for the raising of Lazarus looks like a divine epiphany. John 10:40–42 also looks backwards to the relationship of Jesus' and John the Baptist's ministry, whereas 11:45–53 looks forward to the passion. The miracle story itself, 11:1–44, is given on the basis of a traditional story but it is split up into two parts, the preparation for the miracle (11:1–19) and the actual performance (11:33–44). In between these two parts we find two discourses, one with Martha (11:20–27) and one with Mary (11:28–32) which constitute the center of the whole chapter.

All the normal features of the telling of such miracle stories are found in John 11: (1) the situation; 11:1, 3, 5, (2) the delay; 11:6, 11 ff (cf. Mark 5:21–43), (3) underlining of the severity; 11:17–19, (4) Jesus' anger at the mourners (cf. Mark 5:38 f); 11:33 ff., (5) repeated emphasis upon the reality of death; 11:39, (6) the performance of the miracle; 11:43, (7) the demonstration; 11:44. A peculiar element is the names, Mary and Martha and their brother Lazarus (whom one should not identify with the "beloved disciple"). As 11:2 indicates, these names tie this chapter to the opening of the passion narrative (12:1 ff). It is necessary to raise the problem of the miracles of Jesus—not the question of whether such miracles actually happened, for such a question is completely outside of the horizon of the author of this Gospel. Rather, one must discuss the question of the relevance of the miracle for faith. John writes his Gospel on the basis of traditions which contain several stories of miracles, and John 11 reports the most miraculous of these. John recognizes, at the same time, the great dangers of such a tradition about Jesus as a miracle worker. He handles each instance in its own right: John 4 wants to criticize a faith which rests upon miracles (cf. John 4:48!); John 9 wants to show how ridiculous the scepticism of the officials is, but emphasizes that real faith is something more than the belief in miracles. In John 11 the interpretation must also indicate in which way this Gospel comes to terms with the theological problem of the miracle—an act worked by the same Jesus who is to suffer death himself. This makes it especially important to observe the interpretations which the author has added to the traditional story.

The first of these comments occurs in 11:4. The purpose is not that a man should die, but the glorification of the Son of God. That, however, is a paradox, since the Son of God is glorified by the raising of Lazarus which leads to the counsel of Caiaphas (11:50) and subsequently to the death of Jesus; that is the ultimate meaning of the "glorification." In 11:7–10 the disciples object that Jesus is exposing himself to possible danger. Jesus' answer does not point to the limited time before his own death, but speaks of the time of the revelation which is limited by the hours of rejection and judgment (cf. 9:4–5). John 11:16 is the third of these comments. Lazarus' death may enhance the miracle and thus the belief of the disciples (11:15). However, Thomas recognizes that to follow him (i.e., Jesus) leads the disciples into the death that is threatening him. That is paradoxically the "day" which is epitomized by Jesus' death, i.e., his glorification, whereas those who sentence Jesus pronounce their own judgment; they are in the "night" (cf. also 13.30).

The encounter with Martha (11:20–27) centers around an insufficient understanding of Jesus' role as a revealer, even though this includes the knowledge that he has the power to raise the dead (11:22). Jesus' response (11:23) raises a typical Johannine misunderstanding. Martha's statement in 11:24 is a correct formulation of traditional beliefs (cf. 4:23). But life and resurrections are present in Jesus in such a way that the eschatological timetable becomes irrelevant (11:25–26). Martha's final answer now expresses the new confession of the Christian church which recognizes the real presence of fulfilled traditional hopes in Jesus. "Christ" indicates the realization of messianic hopes; "Son of God" refers to Jesus' power of judgment and resurrection (cf. 5:20–26). The encounter with Mary (11:28–32) leads back to the necessity of the miracle. It demonstrates that Martha's confession did not speak about something like a "spiritual" presence of the power of life, since Mary knows that there is a right to the visible and tangible work of God's revelation in this world. It is striking that this encounter ends with the same sentence with which the encounter with Martha began (11:32; cf. 11:21).

The raising of Lazarus (11:33–44) is largely told with the words of the source. Two interpolations express the Evangelist's theological insights. John 11:40 invites us to advance from the belief of Martha to acceptance of the visible documentation of the glory of God. John 11:42, on the other hand, states that the miracle is done for the crowd that they also might believe because such belief leads to an increase in hostility and thus to the completion of Jesus' ministry in his death "for the people." At first, however, the belief of the crowd is such that the Jewish authorities judge correctly: it will lead to a messianic uprising (11:47–

48). The miracle of the raising of Lazarus thus enforces the development towards the crucifixion. That is told in 11:45–53. Its climax is the involuntary prophecy of the high priest that it is better that one man die for the people (11:50). Faith must accept the cross, because it reveals Jesus' dignity and glory, whereas the miraculous documentation is only its paradoxical symbol.

HOMILETICAL INTERPRETATION

Introduction: The theme for this Sunday revolves around the biblical transmutation of the death of the body. It seems to anticipate Easter, but its primary relevance is to the cross, upon which the church now begins to concentrate. Last Sunday the crucifixion was anticipated as the paradoxical answer to expectations of success and earthly glory. On Passion Sunday the cross is seen in its relation to the transformation of death into life.

First Lesson. To produce human life is a gift delegated by God to men and women acting together. The very power to do this has become a problem in the strain of overpopulation on resources, along with modes of living which destroy life at the ecological level, a mounting pressure and abuse which could make sustaining human life impossible. Death itself is a fact, one clearly accepted by biblical religion. Christianity takes it up into its faith so that it is accepted and transformed. Death also is an apt metaphor for the loss of power, of relationship, of future hope. It is here that Ezekiel becomes of interest.

When life has passed the bones are dry. There is no power to produce life in them nor can the environment restore life to them. The emphasis of the First Lesson is not on individual death but on the disintegration of Israel as a people, a nation. Restoration is not to be accomplished without the word and initiative of God, here delegated to the prophet. Only God can open the grave of exile (death is in a real sense exile—from the known land, the familiar ways—and exile is death). Only God can bring the dead out again, put flesh on the skeleton of their hope, cause them to stand on their own feet, breathe into them the freedom of movement, restore their functioning in life. "I, the Lord, have spoken and will act." For that we can only wait until the word is spoken, the Spirit moves.

It seems to many of our contemporaries that death is an end, an exit into nothingness, resurrection a myth, a wish-fulfillment, an illusion that itself has died. It means a loss of faith in God, for the belief in the possibility of the gift of new life is faith in God, not faith in resurrection—the Bible does not know "immortality" as a continuing of some aspect of human nature or of a divine spark within. It is (note the exegesis) a new creation. To believe in God is to believe in a God who raises the dead, who can, if he wills, deal even with dessicated bones, and the faith is that he does will to do so, when he wills to do so. His creative independence and initiative and act of grace are seen in both creation and new creation. The new creation makes the old the living vehicle of a new spirit.

Second Lesson. This sense that God has acted, that there is a new situation, that the new creation has been initiated, dominates Paul's treatment here. It is something of this sense of newness, of release, of joyful celebration if only by anticipation, that is ultimately to be conveyed to the people. How necessary such a new conceiving of life as Christian, as utterly new, is in the twentieth century! Here then perhaps is the place to begin—not as something wished-for, therefore to be accepted, but to show how, without it, all that civilization can do is to further dessicate the bones. We owe no debt to "the flesh" (the bones are dry and have contributed nothing to us), the flesh of satisfaction of physical desires, whether by bodily acts with nothing sacramental about them, by commercial technology no matter how enticingly advertised, by promise of success with people-manipulation, or the achievement of increasing leisure. Such resources are not essentially creative of new life.

The new life available, known already to the Christian (if not vitally, in feeling and action), is a new state of being, the realization of our baptism in essence. There, symbolically, we have already died and been buried, raised up and given a new spirit. To "become what we are" (sacramentally) is one way to put it but it sounds a cliché and may be misleading. Does Paul say it better?

It is first of all a new relationship. Death may be defined as the loss of relationship—the cessation of all response or ability to respond, to the physical world, of course, but also to people. The essence of grief is the deprivation of the means of relationship. To be led by the Spirit (pledged to us in baptism) is not possible without relatedness, indeed it is demonstrated by the active entering into relationship already given, there to be realized, a relationship to God, to people. One might not be wrong to say the Spirit is the relationship.

What terms can be used for this last other than those that Paul uses? The disintegration, even the denigration, of the "nuclear family" makes such terms ambiguous for some "sons" (and daughters.) Something more than children, produced, given life, set into the world—which is, of course, true of all humans. Something more is intended by "sonship." We share the "Sonship" of Christ. That is, we "come of age," come to the point where we enter into our inheritance. Already we are, in Christ, heirs, though the full enjoyment of the inestimable wealth of that inheritance lies ahead (here we need Paul's words in Gal. 3:23–4:7 as background and the reiterated emphasis on the extent of the "riches" in Ephesians). Put in terms of life, right now at the core (so to speak) of our dying body of flesh there is (as it were) a new body, already born, gaining in life and strength which triumphs over death. If resurrection is to be anticipated, so is death. We have much dying we can do, even now, before the body fails. Advance in Christian life may be expressed as a repeated discovery of new areas of life to which we need to "die" (cease to respond to them) and thus find opened up new areas in which we can "live" (eagerly respond to) and which are not under the dominion of death.

To be conscious of our status as sons and daughters and, therefore, heirs, is to know the Spirit, and the reverse is also true. So that, in unison with our fellow Christians, we recognize, we give voice to, the family-word "Father." So the praise of, the appeal to, God as Father is the keynote of the Christian fellowship, the hint of its life-ahead, the reality and immeasurable extent of its shared expectation. It is this we gather to celebrate. We go out again to extend it to others. As Paul observed, it transcends, in this very connection, all the age-weary barriers of sex and culture and even "religion" (Gal. 3:28).

It is completely misunderstood if thought of as escape from one bondage into another, from one law demanding obedience-by-rote to another. It has all the difference, measured in terms of freedom, between the slave and the heir. In our culture we do not (apparently) have slaves. But are we not enslaved in all kinds of ways, by patterned life, by seeming dependence on contrivances, by opportunities restricted by concentrations of power and by industrial and urban conglomeration, to say nothing of newly understood psychological forms of bondage? Not to fall into any other bondage is the essence of our new relationship. For this new life, mature in Christ, is freeedom in its highest, its most profound sense, to which all other freedoms are but play-anticipation, graded exercises, essential though they are in corporate living.

The Spirit is the motivating power, bringing into life-relationship that Spirit (see exegesis) given us in our baptism to make us over into truly living people, sons and daughters with an inheritance, "imperishable, undefiled, and unfading, kept in heaven for you . . ." (1 Peter 1:14, another address to the newly baptized). In view of this, suffering of any kind comes to weigh less and less in the balance. To take it into the experiencing of life and not be defeated (as Christ did) is a pledge, a "down-payment"—without any element of a transaction—on future glory. Death is still a reality but death has been dethroned, stripped of its tyrannical power, and made a servant, a means of entry into life.

Gospel. Just as Ezekiel's story must not be taken to refer to resurrection in the full sense, so the story of Lazarus' reinstatement in (present) life must not be so taken, not treated as a "sign" in the wrong sense. In reality only one "sign" dominates the Gospel. For what truly manifests the glory of the Christ of the Fourth Gospel is his death on the cross. The very words become transmuted. His "lifting up" (on the cross) becomes in reality (in "very truth") his "lifting up" to the ultimate seat of power and glory in the universe. The "raising" of Lazarus, far from clinching all claims, appears to the establishment as the final threat and leads to Jesus' arrest and death. (Note the short form of the Gospel, vv. [45–] 47–53.)

The longer narrative needs to be taken into account. From the beginning there is the wrestling with death in the standard framework of a miracle-story. Here, in the Johannine format, death as human beings know it and as they experience its shocks is presented. There is a warm, intimate relationship, threatened by terminal illness, and there is Jesus' re-evaluation of it as a means of the glorification of "the Son."

The last phrase is then related to the historic passion. For Jesus to return to Judea means, as the disciples sense, his death. Thomas sensed it most of all and calls on the rest to share Jesus' fate by going with him. All becomes inevitable by the last section of the Gospel. The problem here is to center on death as, so to speak, functional to life. It is a Jesus who is subject to death who deals with people subject to death. The problem is not solved by bringing Lazarus back to temporary life but by Jesus' entry through death into victory over death. The Johannine "hour," the moment of revelation, is not struck when Lazarus emerges from the tomb, but it does strike when Jesus goes forward to the cross (12:27–28).

Martha functions here to state the common problem of death, loss, and grief. She admirably underlines the inability of a general belief in eventual resurrection to solve the problem. Martha's "I know that . . ." is the bereaved's despair at all offers of comfort including religious clichés which speak of an eventual resolution beyond the period to be endured, the now, where the real problem lies. This is not only the last in the series of signs but embodies one of the great "I am" declarations. Jesus had brought the final reality into the present. It is relationship with him that anticipates the new life-in-relation which is the only answer to death, because he did not "spurn" birth as a human and then would not "spurn" death as a human. Without that happening and ending his humanity, his sharing our lot, his complete identification with us would be unreal.

But where Martha begins Mary also ends. In truth there is no easy (or "cheap") comfort. A "miracle" which brings only a temporary solution, dealing only with immediate aspects, is not enough to express the reality of God's redemption. With Martha and Mary we are still that side of the cross. A solution to their problem is not possible, in God's revelation, without a solution of the problem for all people.

We have seen many people die, we have shared the grief which is the common human lot, we experience (to use Alvin Toffler's term) the "future shock" of our own inevitable death and the loss it will entail upon others—but we have not yet seen Jesus die. The death of Christ and the resurrection experience of the living Lord are the determinative fact, and that is the theme of the story.

The relationship-in-life is restored to the Mary-Martha-Lazarus menage —for the time being. In reality we can say Lazarus is restored only that he might share with them the drama of Jesus' crucifixion! Jesus has said that his words (vv. 40–42a) were intended to enable the crowd, those not personally involved at the moment, to believe.

It is the paradox of the gospel that "history" as men's involvement in events must operate if Jesus' intention is to be realized. "For all the people" is the topsy-turvy clue to the closing passage (which may be read alone, but assumes the rest). The judgment of the high priest, endorsed by the action of the council, is that it is better that one man should die (even if unjustly) rather than that all the people should "perish"—that is, lose their place, their hopes, their entity as a people, in effect die themselves corporately (see exegesis on Ezekiel, above). This is the "expediency" of the world, the wisdom-in-emergency of the "flesh." It is the Evangelist who, writing from this (our) side of the cross and resurrection, transforms the sense of the high priest's judgment into a prophecy that the death of Jesus would serve to redeem not only the nation but all the children of God. Jesus' acceptance of suffering ("unto death, even death on a cross," Phil. 2:8) is really all we can know about suffering—that Jesus' faith was confirmed, that God could somehow take suffering into his purpose of love and redemption. And that is true of death, that God can take, has taken, death into his purposes, indeed into his own experience, and not be defeated by it but has made it the gateway to life, life in God's sense.

Nothing less will serve, no temporary alleviation, no postponement, no clichés about God's will or wait and see, but only the present experience of the once-born-once-died Christ as a reality. This reality transcends life and death separation and makes of it a parenthesis in the eternal relationship in which all the sons-daughters of God animated by the Spirit have already the anticipated experience of their inheritance of life, life itself, life-in-very-truth, life indeed.

So we are invited to approach the cross—which denies, distorts, denigrates humanness itself—as the final limit of the Son of God's experience of human-being-ness, by which it is confirmed that he is not "unable to sympathize with our weaknesses" who "himself has suffered and been tested" and so "partaking of the same nature" he might "through death destroy him who has the power of death" and deliver us who "through fear of death were subject to lifelong bondage" (see Hebrews 4:15; 2:14–15, etc.). For the "disassociative" threat of death is the basic and final enemy to freedom and, as we have seen in various ways in this cycle of Lenten Lessons, it is release into freedom that is the essence of salvation, release into that freedom of the sons and daughters of God in the presence of the living Christ and in the community of the Holy Spirit by which we claim our inheritance of the Father's love. So we are prepared to enter more fully into the "memorial" and "anticipation" which is Passiontide and Easter as a truly sacramental experience and the preacher, paradoxically, is reduced to exclaiming, "Thanks be to God for his inexpressible gift."